Boomers *into* Business

How Anyone Over 50 Can
Turn What They Know into Dough
Before and After Retirement

Boomers
into
Business

How Anyone Over 50 Can
Turn What They Know into Dough
Before and After Retirement

Lisa Orrell, CPC

The Promote U Guru
Branding Expert • Marketing Maven • Success Coach
Professional Speaker & Author

Intelligent Women Publishing
A Wyatt-MacKenzie Imprint

Other Books Written by Lisa Orrell

Millennials into Leadership: The Ultimate Guide for Gen Y's Aspiring to Be Effective, Respected, Young Leaders at Work (2009, Intelligent Women Publishing, a Wyatt-MacKenzie Imprint)

Millennials Incorporated: The Big Business of Recruiting, Managing and Retaining the World's New Generation of Young Professionals (2008, Intelligent Women Publishing, a Wyatt-MacKenzie Imprint)

Dedication

This book is dedicated to all the Boomers who are ready and willing to take control of the next chapter of their personal, professional and financial lives with excitement, enthusiasm, and heart! And, I'd also like to dedicate this book to my amazing family: Jenner (my wonderful son), my Mother, my Dad (Stan the Man), Adrienne, Julie, and Ma & Pa Jones. Plus, I'd like to send a special shout out to Team O!

Boomers into Business:
How Anyone Over 50 Can *Turn What They Know Into Dough*
Before & After Retirement

By Lisa Orrell, CPC

FIRST EDITION

ISBN: 9781936214440

Library of Congress Control Number: 2011932539

Intelligent Women Publishing
A Wyatt-MacKenzie Imprint

Acknowledgments

I would like to express my deepest gratitude to the following fabulous experts for their willingness to contribute extremely valuable content to this book. I'm sending you all big hugs for your help and support in gettin' it done!

These generous individuals have been listed in the order that they "appear" inside this book: Sherry Prescott-Willis, Branding & Marketing Expert; Jessica Northey, SocialMediologist; Eve Mayer Orsburn, CEO of Social Media Delivered (.com); Mirna Bard, Founder of NuReach Global; Lynn Baldwin-Rhoades, Founder of both Marketing Shebang and Power Chicks International; David Steel, President of The Steel Method; Bill Graham-Reefer, President of WorldView PR; Susan Young, President of Get in Front Communications, Inc.; Jim Palmer, The Newsletter Guru; Lee B. Salz, Founder and CEO of Business Expert Webinars; Pamela Cox, President of Pamela Cox Email Marketing; Kathleen Gage, Founder of The Street Smarts Marketing System; Vicki Flaugher, Online Marketing Strategist; Diane Marie Pinkard, Sales Guru & Trainer; and Sponsorship Expert, Linda Hollander, the Wealthy Bag Lady.

I'd also like to express lots of thanks to Debbie Feldstein, my amazing Editor. She's the Principle of Creative Blocks Editorial Services (CreativeBlocks.com) in New York City. This is the second book she's helped me with and I adore her. You da bomb, baby!

And, finally, I'd like to send a HUGE virtual hug to my Publisher, Nancy Cleary, President of Wyatt-MacKenzie Publishing, Inc. This is our third book together and she ROCKS!

TABLE OF CONTENTS

PART FOUR
Promote U & Increase Your Income Thru Other Cool Tools

PART FIVE
All about Lisa Orrell, The Promote U Guru

What People Say About *Boomers into Business*

"I just turned 60 and decided to pursue my dream of becoming a Certified Disability Life Coach in my mid-50s. I had been an employee my whole career and I wanted to create my own business so that I could generate more income now, and past 65, doing something that I loved. I hired Lisa to consult with me one-on-one and her wisdom has helped propel my business forward. And, I learned more helpful strategies to expand my business offerings by reading *Boomers into Business!*"

> — *Nancy Bauser, ACSW, BCETS, BCDT,* Trauma Recovery Expert, www.SurvivorAcceptance.com, Author of *Accept, Survive & Thrive – Helping people with disabilities accept themselves and their new life circumstances*

"I'm now 50, a single mom with a teenage son, and I've worked at Title Insurance Companies for over 20 years. I currently don't have enough money to retire comfortably in my 60's and have been trying to figure out what I can do to increase my income on-the-side of my day job. *Boomers into Business* was a godsend! It opened my mind to possibilities I had never thought of and I'm now developing ideas for an expert platform and part-time consulting business that I can do for many years. This will provide me with the additional income I need to be more comfortable now, and later, in life."

> — *Kathy F., San Jose, CA*

"A friend of mine gave me a copy of *Boomers into Business* and it was one of the most valuable gifts I've ever received! I am 62, don't have a college degree, and have worked in a variety of very physical construction jobs pretty much my whole life. I have never been an entrepreneur, but this book gave me the courage to think like that because it provided ideas I could relate to. I never thought I could turn my hobby into a career but now I realize I can, and this book explained how."

> — *Carlos A., Fort Lauderdale, FL*

"As a Boomer in my 60s, Lisa's book topic really hits home for me. Plus, I've hired Lisa as my personal Coach & Consultant and have attended her workshops; always being amazed at this smart, direct and strategic woman! From her depth of experience, she delivers a wealth of tools and guidance designed *to take you from where you are to where you want to be.* I recommend this great book to all you Boomers who are planning the next chapter of your professional lives!"

— *Marilyn Fahrner: Self-employed,* Wealth Building & Business Coach, www.marilynfahrner.com

"I am so bored with what I do for a living, but I've been stuck in a corporate rut for years because, other than going to another company in the same role, I didn't know what else to do. Plus, I'm pushing 55, and I know for a fact I don't have enough in my retirement account and savings to be able to stop working at 65. After I read *Boomers into Business* it gave me the kick I needed to think outside of my 'safe box.' Now I'm developing a topic expert platform that taps into my 30 years of career experience and people have already expressed wanting to hire me for speaking engagements and private consulting. I'm excited about my career, future, and finances for the first time in MANY years."

— *Linda B., Eugene, OR*

"As a (newly) self-employed Boomer who is an Online Business Manager in the Internet Marketing world, I've been following Lisa's tips and strategies as she offers them through her blog and Fan Page posts for quite a while. I always learn something new and I'm able to implement them for myself, and my clients, quickly with excellent results. Thank you, Lisa, for your clear thinking and can-do writing style—I read your monthly tips as soon as they come in and your new book has given me great ideas for expanding my business to generate more on-going income into the future!"

— *Cindy Morus: Self-employed,* Online Business Manager, www.CindyMorus.com

"Women over fifty are looking to *live lives* that matter, whether in the workplace or elsewhere. For those who choose to become self-employed, this is a practical, thorough guide that will help women (and men!) match their talents, strengths, skills, values and vision to careers that can ensure both their emotional and financial well-being."

> — *Kathleen Vestal Logan,* Speaker, Co-author with Betsy Smith, Ph.D.,
> of *Second Blooming for Women: Growing a Life That Matters after Fifty,* www.secondbloomingforwomen.com

INTRODUCTION

One Boomer is Retiring Every 8 Seconds: But Can They Afford To?

Hello! Welcome to my book (now your book)! This is my third book, however it's the first to kick-off my new *The Promote U Guru Guide to...*book series. I plan to roll out quite a few books in this series. All of them will be focused on different aspects of marketing, branding, PR, Social Media, sales and business-building...basically, any topic I can think of that will help self-employed people build their brands, businesses, and income.

Why am I passionate about this? I have been a *self-employed* branding and marketing expert for over 20 years. I received a Bachelor's Degree in Advertising and then started my first advertising agency when I was 25. So I've been getting paid to help individuals and companies build their brands and grow their businesses for a long time. And, because I've been in the business owner "trenches" for over two decades myself, I can relate to my clients on many levels outside of just their marketing challenges.

Now, you may be wondering why I decided to kick-off my series with a book specifically for you, a Baby Boomer. The answer to that is really quite simple. Did you know that according to a special report entitled *Next Generation Leaders: Competency Deficits and The Bridge to Success* by Judy Chartrand, Ph.D. and Bonnie Hagemann, Baby Boomers are currently retiring at the rate of 1 every 8 seconds? And this massive retirement trend has just started!

That's a HUGE amount of people leaving the workforce daily, and is why employers are starting to panic. But that's a whole different topic and one that I'm paid to speak about under my "other" brand where, to the corporate and academic worlds, I'm known as *The Generations Relations Expert* (www.TheOrrell-Group.com). Yes, you are allowed to have more than one brand platform, one career, and one interest. I'm proof of that.

Anyway, back to the reason behind this book. Due to the economic shifts in our country the past couple of years, many Boomers cannot afford to fully retire securely or comfortably when, and as, they'd hoped...regardless of whether they've been an employee their entire career or self-employed.

Did you read the back cover of this book? Well, even if you did, I'm going to repeat some startling stats that I included there: According to *The EBRI Retirement Readiness Rating*™ in 2010:

47.2% of older Boomers (56-62) are at risk of outliving their retirement savings. And 43.7% of younger Boomers (46-55) are at risk of not having enough money for basic monthly expenses when they retire.

47.2%??? That's almost half of Boomers 56 to 62! Those statistics are staggering. It means we have millions of people who cannot afford to stop working at 65 and are currently seeking ways to make more income now and on an on-going basis past 65.

But, on the other end of that spectrum, there are Boomers who simply don't want to fully retire, *even if they can*, and are looking for something different to do.

Another scenario I see a lot are younger Boomers in their early-50's, ten to fifteen years away from "standard" retirement age, totally bored with what they're doing professionally, and wanting to make a career change now. They truly can't fathom staying in their current occupation for another one or two decades and they, too, are seeking options.

I'm assuming there's a good chance you fall into one of the categories I just described or you wouldn't be reading this book. And I'm also assuming that, like many other Boomers, you'd prefer the next chapter of your professional life be as a self-employed person because you've been "working for the man (or woman)" for a very long time.

Or perhaps you're already self-employed and you may want to remain so, but you also want to generate more income. Or perhaps you want to do something different, too. I get a lot of self-employed people who come to me in their 50's and 60's, bored with what they're doing after 30+ years! Beyond boredom, some of them have physically challenging jobs that they know they can't keep doing for another 10-20 years. But they need to keep working, so they're looking for options…and working as a "greeter" at a local 'big box' store doesn't thrill them.

Here's the bottom line: I have helped countless individuals launch their "expert" platforms or improve their current branding platforms and businesses. And many of these clients have been 50+. So I totally understand that you are probably trying to figure out "how and what" is in your future professionally. If I'm correct, please keep reading…you picked up the right book!

And I'd like to get something straight right away: This book does not outline a "get rich quick" program. It is not another bogus book with an angle like: *How to Make $100 Million Dollars in Real Estate with No Money in 5 Days.* The only way real estate even relates to this book is if you're a realtor who is a Boomer, and you want to expand on your brand to make more money (or make a career change).

This book is a legitimate "how to" guide written specifically for Boomers who: take their financial futures seriously; have an entrepreneurial spirit (or have always wanted one!); want to re-invent themselves; or who are currently self-employed and want to increase their income.

As the subtitle of this book says, we're going to explore how to *turn what you know into dough,* and set you on a path to *develop a new career* or expand on your *current* one. And the ultimate goal here is for you to generate on-going income, full-time or part-time, doing something that is flexible, interesting, *and possible to do into your golden years.*

The good news is that just about ANY Boomer is qualified to embark on this journey without much money! Seriously, you can launch an *expert platform* with little more than a basic website and a lot enthusiasm. I know people who have done it for under $500 bucks and within a short time were making a significant income and having a great time!

And, in case you were wondering, having a college degree or high school diploma doesn't matter. It's all about attitude, branding, and desire.

So, whether your career path for the past 25+ years has been as a corporate executive, a homemaker, a jewelry maker, a gardener, a house painter, a therapist, a butcher, baker, or candlestick maker, or whatever…you possess knowledge that people need…and they will pay you for what you know!

Even if you've simply had a particular hobby for many years, it means you have skills and knowledge that can be developed into a new career where people will seek your expertise…and they will pay you for what you know!

OR perhaps you've had interest in something you don't know much about. You'll learn strategies that can get you up-to-speed quickly on that topic so you can position yourself as an "expert" fast…and they will pay you for what you know! (Are you sensing a pattern here?)

But, are you unclear on WHAT that area of expertise could be? Not sure HOW you can make an income from it? Not sure WHERE to get started? Don't panic! That's what *Boomers into Business* is for!

In this book you'll learn "what" you can do with the experience or interests you have, and "how" to create your brand platform and positioning. You'll also learn the marketing, PR, and business strategies to "make it happen." And NO previous marketing or business experience is required…you'll read proof of that shortly!

The only thing you need is an open mind, the desire to make a change, the courage to do it, and some guidance. This book can provide the guidance, but the rest is up to you.

Oh, and one last thing before we jump into Chapter One. Although I personally use, or have used, just about every strategy discussed in this book myself, and I educate my clients and audiences about them, this book is not "The Lisa Show." I reached out to quite a few brilliant colleagues who are experts in specific strategies we'll be discussing. And, being the fabulous people they are, they each contributed a chapter that pertained to their area of expertise.

This is great for you! It means you'll be getting a lot of helpful tips, advice and strategies from *different* experts—not just from yours truly.

Ready?

It's time to start changing YOUR financial future, have fun, and focus on *Boomers into Business!*

Note: If you're interested in receiving a free copy of the complete 2010 EBRI.org report mentioned in this Introduction, here's the info: *The EBRI Retirement Readiness Rating™ Retirement Income Preparation and Future Prospects* by Jack VanDerhei and Craig Copeland, Employee Benefit Research Institute (EBRI.org).

Promote U Thru
Brand Building

"A brand that captures your mind gains behavior.
A brand that captures your heart gains commitment."

~ Scott Talgo, World-Renowned Brand Strategist

INTRODUCTION TO PART ONE

In this section, I'm going to get your brain thinking about what you can do to increase your income based on your career experience, strengths, and/or interests. And for those of you who are self-employed already, you'll learn how to make a career change, or expand your current business offerings, in ways you probably haven't considered before.

As I mentioned in the Introduction, you have expertise and knowledge that other people are willing to pay for. The key is to position *you* as an "expert" and create the strategies and offerings to make it happen. Then, once you've determined your "expert platform" (who you are and what you'll offer), you must determine how you want to be known and perceived. And that is all about *branding.*

Even if you are currently self-employed and feel you have a good brand platform, you won't want to skip this section. Why? Because you may want to add to what you currently offer (which could affect your current branding), AND you may learn how to improve your current branding.

I will tell you that 80% of the self employed people who hire me and who have been self-employed for quite some time, need their branding improved. Aside from poor marketing, their *poor branding* is affecting their ability to generate the revenue they desire...and that is ultimately affecting their future financial security.

Branding is a weird animal. What it is, what it isn't, how to create one, and how to promote one, are topics that have baffled millions of people and millions of companies (large and small) forever. Like I just mentioned before, branding is where a lot of clients I work with fall short...many of them have done nothing to create a *unique* brand that sets them apart from their competition because they are honestly confused about who they are.

Basically, you <u>can'</u>t create and execute effective marketing, Social Media, sales and PR strategies, <u>or a solid business plan</u>, until you know "WHO" you want to be, "WHAT" you want to offer, and "HOW" you are different. So let's jump into Chapter One! This will all make a lot more sense shortly!

CHAPTER ONE
How to Turn What You Know Into Dough

By Lisa Orrell

I think that the best way to get your mind going in the right direction for determining *how to turn what you know into dough* is to provide you with some inspirational examples. I encourage you to have a pen and paper handy because as you read, you are likely to come up with ideas for yourself that you will want to jot down.

Are You Now Or Have You Ever Been A…

Corporate HR Executive: You can become a Consultant and "**HR Topic Expert**" who advises small and medium-sized businesses that don't have an HR person on staff, on proper HR practices, rules and regulations. You can also offer your services as an *interim* **(freelance) HR Manager** for companies that need your knowledge and services on a part-time basis until they have grown enough to require a full-time, permanent employee in that role.

And you can make additional income by **conducting seminars, webinars and workshops for small business owners on important HR practices** they need to know to avoid legal issues with employees. Business owners are not "born" with this knowledge, so you can be the expert that educates them…and they'll pay you!

Plumber: You can expand your offerings outside of just providing your normal fix-it services by becoming a "**Do It Yourself Plumbing Expert**" for homeowners. And, if you want, you can even choose to drill that down to an even more targeted niche of "Do It Yourself Plumbing Expert for *Female* Homeowners."

As such, you can conduct "do it yourself" presentations, as well as **private training for individuals**, on how to make basic repairs or upgrades in their home (i.e., installing a new toilet, putting in new faucets, repairing a dripping shower, etc.).

There are many homeowners and *new* rental property owners with tight budgets. They would be willing to pay to attend your presentations or hire you for private training sessions because it would save them money in the long run because they wouldn't have to hire someone to do the job for them!

Also, you can gain recognition and generate income from your "topic expert" branding by **speaking at home improvement expos and at local hardware or home improvement stores in your area.**

This can also lead to developing products to sell such as how-to videos, books, e-guides, etc... We'll be discussing that strategy in more depth shortly.

Gardener & Landscaper: This is a true story. A colleague told me about an elderly man who had been a gardener for *35 years.* He was the typical neighborhood gardener who had simply "mowed & blowed" yards for homeowners throughout his town.

But during his career, he had come up with his irrigation and fertilization strategy for lawns that were brown. He could get just about any sad-looking lawn green and lush fast. And whenever he improved one neighbor's brown lawn, all the other neighbors who had brown lawns hired him to make theirs green again, too.

One of his clients suggested that he start conducting presentations for homeowners, rental property owners, and *other* gardeners on his amazing method. So he took this advice, and it led to speaking engagements at large gardening and irrigation industry events and home and garden expos, as well as being interviewed by industry and home improvement media.

Basically, this man went from being a neighborhood gardener—who was starting to struggle physically (thus financially) due to aging—into becoming a "rock star" in the gardening, lawn care, and irrigation worlds. And, it was all because he leveraged his "fixing brown lawn" expertise and promoted himself as THE expert for fixing them.

Sound a little odd? Well, he **tripled his income in one year**, left behind the daily physical grind of being a gardener for other people, worked less hours, became a "celebrity" in his industry, and was able to continue as an in-demand expert, speaker and consultant until he was in his 80's. Why? Because many people were willing to pay him, handsomely, for his knowledge and expertise.

College Professor or School Teacher: You can take your expertise and *expand it outside of the classroom.* Perhaps you have been a second grade teacher for 25 years and have an uncanny ability to teach and motivate kids that other teachers, faculty and parents have deemed "impossible." And, you've noticed over the years, that a lot of colleagues and parents have sought your advice.

You can package your expertise into a "topic expert" brand platform that can attract other teachers to seek your consultation. And this can also lead to **conducting paid workshops for teachers** and **paid speaking engagements at industry conferences.**

Plus, you can offer private consultation services for parents wanting your advice about their "impossible" child. Sure, there are child psychologists who do this, but YOUR focus can be on the *child's issue in the classroom.* And this can result in child psychologists wanting to partner with you or referring clients to you.

In short, your expertise can "supplement" the therapy other professionals are providing to parents and/or children. You've worked IN the classroom…many child psychologists haven't. That makes your front-line experience valuable. And people will pay you for it.

College Professors can focus on becoming a known expert on their subject matter. Let's say you're an American History Professor. You can leverage your knowledge on American History in general, or in one specific area of American History (i.e. the Civil War). By promoting yourself as "a leading expert" on the Civil War you can attract **paid speaking engagements, media interviews, and lucrative consulting opportunities with the entertainment industry** on movies, documentaries and books on that topic. You can even make additional income **for paid tutoring sessions** with college students seeking help with their term papers and coursework.

Psychologist, Therapist or Coach: I've had quite a few clients who fall into these professional categories. They often come to me because they are totally burnt-out on just making a living from one-on-one client sessions, and they want to make more money by leveraging their knowledge into a topic expert brand platform.

Here's one example: One client of mine had been a marriage counselor for 25 years. She was tired of doing one-on-one client sessions and was not making enough money for retirement as she entered her late 50's. Therefore, she was also very stressed about her financial future. But she had no idea what to do to generate income outside of one-on-one client sessions.

So we focused on creating a moniker (brand positioning) for her that was catchier than "marriage counselor" (there are thousands of *those* out there!), and I asked her to **write a short e-book and a series of articles.** Then we developed presentation topics targeted at people who were struggling in their marriages or committed relationships. Very soon afterwards, she was making additional income from conducting paid presentations and she began to attract a lot of media interviews!

Also, in a short period of time, she was able to cut her one-on-one client session bookings in half, *but doubled her income*, despite the fact that she was working less. This all happened because of re-branding herself as a "topic expert" (and not *just* being a marriage counselor), and by adding speaking engagements and product development to her business model.

We also leveraged her marriage counseling knowledge and created topic ideas that would appeal to employees struggling with their **workforce** relationships. She never realized that she was just as qualified to help with "co-worker relationships" as she was "love relationships." This realization opened up a whole new world for her!

And what was the result of *that* strategic move? Companies began to hire her to conduct seminars and workshops on improving workforce relations and communication. Plus, she made more money for conducting one 2-hour seminar than she did for doing two weeks of individual therapy sessions.

Very quickly, this client went from solely focusing on one-on-one marriage counseling sessions for 25 years (and becoming totally burnt-out), to actually creating an "expert brand" platform that generated more money, and more fun, than she ever thought possible!

Her renewed passion also resulted in financial security and less stress, and provided her with a career shift that she could do, happily, well into her golden year. And by the way, we worked together on this branding change and business model shift <u>when she was 58.</u>

<u>Homemaker</u>: Some very successful female entrepreneurs were stay-at-home moms who came up with amazing ideas to simplify or improve different childcare or homecare tasks, and then marketed their solutions. Others are women who were very career-focused prior to having kids, but chose to become stay-at-home moms and then developed ideas to create a business they could run from home.

But, what if you're in your late 50's or 60's, your kids are now adults, you have been a homemaker for the past 30+ years (focused on everyone else except *you* all those years), and you now want, *or need*, to generate an income?

Needing to generate an income becomes a serious reality for many Boomer homemakers due to: divorce; retirement accounts taking a dive; investments not yielding their anticipated projections; unexpected emergencies draining savings and/or assets; or due to becoming a widow.

So what can <u>you</u> do? Aside from going back to school or enrolling in a vocational program to learn a new skill set (which can take a lot of time and money), you can **focus on the skills you've acquired as full-time homemaker and as an intelligent woman.**

Perhaps you are an amazing cook; have a flair for home decorating; are brilliant at running a house and raising 3 kids on a tight budget; are known among friends and family as a terrific time management and scheduling pro; or have grown the most amazing vegetable garden, or rose garden, in your neighborhood.

Any skills such as those can be turned into a "topic expert" platform where other people *will pay you* for your expertise!

Take a minute to think about The Food Network. Several of the stars on that network did not go to culinary school, didn't own, or even work in, a restaurant, and didn't have professional careers in "food" prior to auditioning. Some of them just had a passion for food and cooking, and decided to audition for the network with the hopes of turning their passion into a profession.

Look back at the example of the gardener I mentioned earlier. Yes, he had been a gardener for a long time. But what ended-up being his topic expert brand platform was his creation of a solution to *make dead lawns healthy again.* He could have just as easily been a weekend gardening enthusiast who developed an amazing solution to revive a lawn or grow fabulous roses.

There are many people out there who, out of a *passion for a hobby* (not an occupation), came up with a solution while doing their hobby, and then promoted themselves as an "expert" to teach that solution to others.

Heck, there are women in their 50's, 60's, 70's and 80+ who are scrapbook junkies and market the ideas they come up with to *other scrapbook enthusiasts.*

The key here is focus on your strengths and interests, and realize that you can "brand" yourself as an expert people will pay to learn from…*even if you haven't had a "professional career" in the workforce for decades!*

Everything I discussed in the examples above is applicable to any career or background: lawyer, dentist, CPA, realtor, consultant, web designer, corporate employee (in any position, from any industry), farmer, short order cook, logger, truck driver, bookkeeper, pastry chef, pilot, scuba diver, homemaker, parent, etc.

Again, the core concept is that you focus on your strengths and interests, and realize that you can create a "brand," or expand your current brand, *and people will pay you for what you know.* And, yes, professionals such as lawyers and CPA's already get paid for their "knowledge and expertise," but I know many with private practices who struggle financially or are bored with what they do. So, they, too, want to expand their brand into an "expert platform" to generate more income by speaking or developing products, and (oftentimes) *to attract more notoriety.*

But What If You Are Not Interested in Leveraging What You Currently Know? What If You Want to Reinvent Yourself As an Expert in a Totally Different Area?

That scenario is a reality for many people. Maybe, just maybe, you want to set off on a whole new course professionally. Well, it's possible and it can happen quickly. Let me illustrate this by sharing my own story.

I had owned my advertising agency in Silicon Valley for about 20 years. I started it when I was just 25 and over time had become very burnt out on running the firm, managing employees, and working with technology companies. But I wasn't sure what I wanted to do in the next chapter of my professional life because owning my agency was really all I had ever done. But I did know that I liked to write and wanted to start speaking more…and I *definitely* knew that I wanted to get paid for both.

While I still owned my agency, I began to research the Millennials (aka. Gen Y) from a marketing perspective. I wanted to know more about them as consumers, what made them tick; and to understand who they were as the new future leaders of our world. And I was doing this because I wanted to be able to educate my clients about them as a "consumer group."

But I noticed whenever I discussed Millennials with my clients and colleagues that just about everyone started discussing them as *employees*: How to recruit them, manage them, retain them, etc. And they'd also start sharing the challenges they had with the Millennials they managed or worked with.

That's when a light bulb went off for me! I saw that there was a need for organizations and front line managers to better understand Millennials as the newest members of the workforce; not just understand them as a new consumer group to sell their products or services to.

So, I wrote my first book, *Millennials Incorporated,* and addressed this topic. I wrote it for companies and managers to enlighten them on how to recruit, manage, motivate, and retain this new generation of young professionals. The book immediately positioned me as an expert about Millennials and generational dynamics in the workplace. And I used the book to launch my paid seminars and workshops, and for attracting tons of media interviews.

I then wrote my second book for the Millennials themselves, *Millennials into Leadership.* It was written to educate them on how to be effective, respected, young leaders in the workforce. My second book also led to paid speaking opportunities at companies and colleges.

But I knew that I didn't want to talk about Millennials, generations, and leadership as my new *full-time* career. I missed using the highly creative side of my brain that had been developed during my long background and passion for marketing. So I decided to launch my Promote U Guru brand and consulting practice to work with individuals on improving their branding, marketing, PR and business building strategies. This was the perfect solution that allowed me to discontinue my agency and step away from working with technology companies after two decades, but still monetize my vast business and marketing experience, and keep my creative juices flowing.

Fast forward to today! I still do a lot of speaking on Millennial and Generations topics for corporations and colleges, but I choose to invest a majority of my time, and I make a majority of my living, as The Promote U Guru.

The take away concept in my story is that YOU can research a niche that you find interesting, but know very little about, and become an expert in it quickly just like I did with Millennials and Generational dynamics! Sure, writing a book can help make that happen, but I know many people who have launched entire topic expert brand platforms by simply writing a short special report, how-to guide, or eBook, or by simply starting a blog.

And FYI, **I wrote my first book in about 4 months.** So if *you* choose to write a book, it doesn't have to be a (painful) one to three year project. You can even hire a ghostwriter to do research and handle most of the "heavy lifting" for you!

Let me put it this way: If you spend just one month heavily researching a particular topic that you're interested in, you will know more about that topic than a majority of the population does. And, yes, there will be people who are also considered experts on that topic, but if you are creative with your branding and positioning, and diligent with your marketing and on-going topic research, *you can also be considered an expert on it* with the ability to generate revenue from your expertise.

Are there other "generations" experts out there who have Ph.D.'s, or who have spent years researching generational dynamics, or who have written books similar to mine and also get paid to speak on the same topics I do? Yes! But there is enough business to go around! And I've been good at marketing and promoting myself as "The Generations Relations Expert" which has led to getting paid to educate others with *my* knowledge in this area.

I received $3,000 for the very first seminar I ever conducted on the topic of "Managing Millennials." A company hired me, paid me, and then re-hired me to present several other seminars and workshops...and the ball kept rolling after that.

I would imagine that most of you wouldn't mind making an extra $1,000 to $5,000+ per month, by conducting 1-2 seminars or workshops every few weeks! And I know topic experts that also decide to get into presenting **keynote speeches** and command fees as high as $7,500+ for doing just <u>one</u> 30-minute speech! These people are not famous; they are simply self-made and self-proclaimed experts on specific topics.

But, if you have no desire to do "public" speaking as part of your revenue stream, <u>don't panic</u>! You can generate significant revenue from your chosen expertise by: Coaching, consulting or training *individuals or small groups*; creating and selling "how to" products, eBooks or special reports; conducting virtual presentations from your home (without having to stand up in front of an audience) via webinars or teleseminars; and a variety of other strategies…many of which will be discussed later in this book.

There are even topic experts who make a great living from only selling ad space in their newsletters or on their blogs…and they never conduct a presentation, travel, or create products. They just write about their area of expertise via a blog or newsletter (or create an e-zine), build a following, and then other people or businesses *pay them for advertising space* to reach their audience. Plus, they can also generate income by writing articles for other blogs, newspapers and magazines.

Okay! I hope Chapter One got your mind racing and ideas pumping. Now we're going to go to the next step that happens *after you've determined what your topic expertise could be*: how to create a *unique* **brand platform** that will enable you stand out from the competition and generate income.

Branding Demystified

By Lisa Orrell

I'd like to kick-off Chapter Two with some *Branding Fast Facts* that you should factor into your thinking:

1. **Most offerings (services or products) have similar quality and features.** Example: You own an ice cream parlor. What makes your scoop shop and the products you sell different from what's down the block? Or you're a Life Coach. What makes you and your advice different...better? Whether you're selling ice cream or Life Coaching services, chances are many of your competitors have similar offerings.
2. **People make buying decisions based on trust.** This means it's important to make one of your main branding "values" honesty and integrity...and to live and breathe those values into everything you say and do with customers and potential customers.
3. **In general, people judge companies 10% by what they say and 90% by how they appear.** So how your marketing materials appear is crucial. This includes everything from your website to your business cards.
4. **"Designed" brands rate stronger on virtually all financial measurements.** What does this mean? Spend some extra dough on getting your marketing materials created by a design professional! Sorry to be the one to tell you this, but people DO judge a book by its cover. And your "cover" as an expert is your website and other marketing materials. *Make them reflect your brand in a professional way!*

When Is a Brand Not A Brand?

Now let's get into what a brand is, *and is not*. I'll start by explaining what a brand is NOT:

1. It's not a logo
2. It's not a website or collateral material
3. It's not your Social Media presence (Twitter, Facebook, LinkedIn, MySpace, etc.)
4. It's not your company name
5. It's not a direct marketing campaign or ad campaign
6. It's not your products

These are all things that <u>support and reflect</u> your brand. *So... what IS a brand?* It is a person's emotional feeling about you, your company and/or your product, and it is a promise for a specific experience.

And your brand *touches everything* pertaining to you and your business, such as: your phone system and your voicemail message; your lobby or storefront; your customer service; your employees; your current and potential customers; your product distribution; and all of your marketing materials and tools (online and off).

A key concept that I strongly recommend burning into your brain is this:

When someone has contact with your brand, one of two things happens: your brand promise is reinforced...or it is weakened.

This is why it is so important to know what your brand value, brand positioning, brand promise, and brand personality are. They need to be reinforced and reflected in everything you say, do, and create.

And, for those of you who have (or will have) employees or contractors, they need to be aware of your brand promise and values, too. As the owner, you're the **brand evangelist**, and that means making sure anyone working for your business focuses on reinforcing your brand...not weakening it.

One of the best things you can do to create a positive brand platform, is focus on being *customer-centric*. Always be open to listening to feedback, have a top-to-bottom commitment to making your customers the #1 priority, and always look at your business decisions from the customer's perspective.

Think about it…you're a customer for a wide variety of companies. Why are YOU loyal to their brand(s)? I bet it's probably because they promise a specific experience with their product or service and consistently deliver on it.

If you can make a person's experience with your brand *consistently* consistent with your brand promise, you are heading down the right path.

CHAPTER THREE

3 Steps to Creating a Unique Brand Platform (with brand 'muscle' exercises)

By Lisa Orrell

I hope after reading Chapter Two you have a better understanding of the concept of branding. Certainly I realize it's not a super simple one; otherwise clients wouldn't hire me to help them with theirs and larger companies wouldn't hire big marketing firms to help them with theirs.

But if you can really focus on what I've shared thus far, and make the effort to follow the info I'll be sharing in this chapter, you CAN create a unique brand platform for yourself. And once you've come up with what you think works, I recommend running your concept by trusted clients, friends and/or colleagues for their honest feedback. Or, if you have employees, consider doing the process as a group effort!

Okay, let's get started on the 3 Steps to Creating a Unique Brand Platform…

STEP ONE: **Define Your Core Business & Determine Your Value Add**

STEP ONE OVERVIEW: This step is to give you the big picture on: *who* you are; *what* your core business is; and what your *value* is. The exercise below is courtesy of my good friend and colleague, Sherry Prescott-Willis, who is also a marketing and branding expert and author. It's from her popular book *MarketThis! An Effective 90-Day Marketing Tool* (www.MarketThisBook.com) and is available on Amazon.

Example: Mobile Mercedes Mechanic (Service Business)

Snapshot of Business: Mobile Mercedes Mechanic is a self-owned mobile mechanic service. The owner has been fixing, repairing, inspecting and working with Mercedes-Benz vehicles for over twenty-five years.

My core business is…

Fixing Mercedes-Benz cars at people's homes with a mechanic who offers a personalized experience for all customers. Customers receive a complete package of good service and years of Mercedes-Benz expertise along with a personality!

My product or service adds value to the customer by providing…

Years of Mercedes-Benz experience with personal touch. Charged by job, not hour, providing a more affordable alternative to doing business directly with a Mercedes-Benz dealership. Customers also receive the added value of an onsite or phone diagnostic consultation.

That helps the customer to….

Feel comfortable and be well informed about the service detail they are getting for their auto.

As a result they…

Have a more personalized experience in location of their choice, and a free educational session on their car, resulting in an overall more positive experience…

…than they would if they did not buy my product or service.

My service is offering…

A more personalized, more affordable and more educational approach

…than my competitors.

STEP ONE EXERCISE: It's Your Turn! Determine Your Core Business & Value

Using the example above as a guide, fill in answers for the following as they relate to you:

- **My core business or expertise is...**

- **My product, service or expertise adds value to my customers by providing...**

- **That helps them (my current or potential customers) to....**

- **As a result they...**

- **...than they would if they did not buy my product, service or expertise.**

- **My service is offering (more/better...)**

- **...than my competitors.**

SUGGESTION: Prior to completing the exercise, I also suggest doing this...

- **List 3-5 qualities that make your product, service, or yourself unique as compared to your competition.**

This can help give you more clarity before doing the exercise.

STEP TWO: How to Define Your Brand Personality

STEP TWO OVERVIEW: Once you know the big picture about your brand from Step One, it's time to apply a *personality* to your brand. That means you'll need to define how you want your brand to be perceived in a unique way. By determining this, you'll impact everything about your brand, such as: your marketing copy, how your marketing materials look, the products you develop, the marketing campaigns you create, the presentation topics you develop, your focus in Social Media, etc.

Here's an example: Apple Computers, Inc. is cool and hip. Period. And that type of *brand personality* permeates into everything they do: The company website, their ad campaigns, even their product development. And I don't just mean how cool their products are from an innovation standpoint; I'm also referring to the *physical* design of them. Their products *look* cool.

Heck, Steve Jobs, the CEO, even looks cool. He does global product announcements in jeans, black turtlenecks and sneakers, not expensive business suits.

This is also a good time to think about your personal *visual* brand. What do I mean by that? Here are a few illustrations for you to chew on: Donald Trump and his hair (he *knows* it is part of his brand, big time); Ellen DeGeneres' sneakers, funky clothes and dancing; and Michael Jackson's infamous sequined single glove.

You can consider a visual brand element that will stand out from the competition and make you memorable. Let's say you love the color red. You could be known for always wearing red shirts/blouses, or red pants, or red shoes, or red socks, red ties, or red hats.

BRAND PERSONALITY EXAMPLES:

Apple: Cool, hip, playful, cutting-edge, fun, irreverent

Happy Hills Motel: Honest, simple, friendly, humble, reliable, unpretentious

The Promote U Guru: Experienced, credible, fun, playful, cool, trustworthy, caring

STEP TWO EXERCISE: It's Your Turn! Now Define Your Brand Personality

MY BRAND IS: Make a list of descriptive words (adjectives) like the examples provided. Don't go 'plain vanilla.' Get creative and go Technicolor!

STEP THREE: How to Create Your Positioning Statement

STEP THREE OVERVIEW: Okay. Now it's time to bring everything from Step One and Step Two together into a cohesive Positioning Statement. Your Positioning Statement becomes the foundation for your branding efforts: visual, written, and verbal. Typically, your positioning statement is an internal-use-only tool, but everything will spin from it. This is NOT your Mission Statement. And it's not meant to read like a clever headline on an ad. It is supposed to be a straightforward statement that defines the essence of your business—who you are, who your audience is, and your point of differentiation. This will make more sense when you read the examples below.

POSITIONING STATEMENT EXAMPLE #1: Happy Hills Motel

To budget minded travelers, Happy Hills Motel is the comfortable, friendly place to stay that is always the lowest price of any major motel chain.

POSITIONING STATEMENT EXAMPLE #2: The Promote U Guru

To small business owners, solo practitioners, speakers and authors, The Promote U Guru is the experienced Branding Expert, Marketing Consultant and Success Coach who helps clients build their brands and improve their marketing quickly and affordably, while having fun in the process.

STEP THREE EXERCISE: It's Your Turn! Now Create Your Positioning Statement

Write 3 different Positioning Statements for your business. Follow the formula provided and fill in the parenthesis with your info:

The Formula for Creating Your Positioning Statement
To (target market), Brand X (your company, name or moniker) is the (frame of reference) that (point of difference).

Alllrighhhtyyy! That concludes Chapter Three. If you follow the 3 steps provided, you will be much closer to creating, or improving, a unique Expert Branding Platform. And, again, this is the foundation for all of your marketing and business efforts, so it's critical! You can't effectively create your marketing materials, promote what you offer, and express why you're different, if you aren't clear on *who you are!*

Okay, now let's discuss what you need to get your business up and running…

CHAPTER FOUR
The Basic Branding & Business Tools You Need to Succeed

By Lisa Orrell

I realize that some of you already own a business and are reading this book because you want to expand your brand and offerings to increase your income. Therefore, you probably already have many branding and business tools in place. If this describes you, then you'll want to make sure that if you plan to add speaking or other services and products to your offerings, the information about those are added to your website and your other marketing materials. You'll also want to revisit your Business Plan and map out your new goals and ideas.

But for those you who will be getting started on a new career path and don't have any branding and business tools developed, here are the *basic* items you'll need to launch professionally:

Your Business Plan: Once you've determined that you want to start a full-time or part-time career as a topic expert, or expand your current business by *becoming* a recognized topic expert, you'll want to get your thoughts down on paper. And that is called a Business Plan.

A business plan gives you the opportunity to map out your ideas, strategies, budget needs, competitive landscape, and operational considerations. It is a "living" document that will **evolve over time** as your business evolves.

You want to create and maintain a business plan so that you remain knowledgeable about the internal and external factors that can impact your success.

Smart small business owners revisit their business plans on a regular basis and make adjustments to them based on new economic conditions, industry fluctuations, and shifts in their personal/professional goals and interests.

But my intention here is not to outline all the details of what goes into a business plan. There are entire books available JUST on that topic! My goal is to emphasize that you should create one before you fully immerse your time, energy and resources into launching your new, or modified, business venture.

A free, reliable and credible resource that clearly explains how to create a comprehensive business plan, and that also provides helpful information for starting a small business, is the U.S. Small Business Administration. Check out their website at SBA.gov to support your journey!

Your Business Name: I recommend that you make "you" your brand, and not come up with a name that is obscure like Pluto Consulting Services...unless your name is 'Pluto' that is. If you *do* want a business name that will be the **front brand**, then make sure your name is in it to support **you as the brand** (like Jones Consulting Company or Sally Smith Coaching).

But, again, I recommend that you only come up with a company name to use for your business bank account, taxes, and to have an entity that clients can write checks to (so they are not writing them to you personally). You want to have separate bank accounts for personal and business, and you'll need to get a business license in your county. Your business name will be used for those "behind the scenes business things."

The point here is that, as a topic expert, people will be coming to you and not a company name, so don't "hide" behind an obscure company name. Remember, as a topic expert, *you are the brand!*

For example, my main web address is PromoteUGuru.com (my brand/moniker), and I have LisaOrrell.com redirect to that. But I have a separate business entity name that is not promoted publicly and it's used for client payments, bank accounts and taxes. My company's name is *not* "Promote U Guru"; that's how I position myself to the public.

Your Logo: I created a logo for Promote U Guru, and have had logos for my previous businesses. So even if you decide to make your branding your name (JoeDingle.com) you can still have a logo designed to stylize your name and moniker/title (i.e. Joe Dingle:

The Green Lawn Guru). This logo will then be used on your website, business cards and marketing materials. If you go this branding/naming route, your *behind-the-scenes* business entity name can then be something basic, and not publicized, so you won't need a logo for it.

If you can't afford to hire a graphic designer, there are several online services you can go to for inexpensive logo design. Here are 2 popular ones that I'm assuming will still be available when you read this:

- LogoMaker.com: This service provides tons of icons and fonts to choose from and you can create your own logo for around $50 bucks.

- LogoTournament.com: With this service, you set the price you're willing to pay, fill out an online form with info the designers need to know, and then tons of freelance designers post designs for you to review. The designer whose logo you choose is the person who gets paid. I have had several clients use this service and for around $250 they each received over 30 really good logos to choose from!

Your Website: This is your brand's most important marketing tool. And you don't want to start creating one until you're clear on your branding because that will impact the messaging you put on the site, as well as impact how it looks. Also, you want to do your logo design first because the colors used on the logo will establish the color palette to be used for your website and your other marketing materials. To create an effective, professional brand presence *visually*, you want to make sure your colors, fonts and logo are consistent on ALL of your marketing materials!

Another reason you want to create your logo first is because it may include a cool icon in it that can be used as a main graphic element in your website's design. An example of this is the Nike® "swoosh." Their swoosh icon is often used separately as a standalone graphic element (without the company name next to it).

Memorable…high impact…no 'name' required.

Just like logo design, there are tons of do-it-yourself website design solutions available. However, if you <u>can</u> afford it, I strongly recommend hiring a professional web designer who has a strong portfolio and great references. Your website will oftentimes be the FIRST point of contact someone has with your brand and, as I mentioned before, *people do judge a book by its cover!* So make sure it's professional, user-friendly, has no glitches in functionality, and reflects you as a leading expert.

At the time of this writing, Wordpress has gained huge popularity as a web development platform. Both of my websites were custom designed on that platform and I love it because I can make content changes myself, thus saving me money on monthly web maintenance. (Coding knowledge is not required for basic content updates).

But if you can't afford to hire a web designer to create a custom website for you, there are thousands of existing Wordpress templates (referred to as "themes") you can choose from to create your own website. Some of them are free and some of them have to be purchased (ranging from $10 to $1000+). You can even provide an existing template to a webmaster to build the site for you and that can be much cheaper than having a website designed from scratch.

Word of caution: If you do hire a webmaster, don't rely on them to be a "marketing strategist." Many of them simply know how to make websites look nice and build them. But they typically don't know how to consult on what your main navigation should include and the features your home page and internal pages should have.

I'd say 90% of the clients who come to me have websites that need work. They either look horrible, or the copy is terrible and unclear, or they look nice but important navigation tabs and features are missing. So one of the first things we do is tackle fixing the website. The goal is to make the website as effective as possible before your start working on driving traffic to it.

My advice is to hire someone like me for even just 1-2 hours of web strategy consultation before you or a webmaster start design. That minimal investment in consultation can save you a lot of money, time, and headaches in the long run.

Your SEO (Search Engine Optimization): It doesn't do you any good to have a website if no one can find it when doing Internet keyword searches. "If you build it, they will come" may work for Kevin Costner in *Field of Dreams*, but you'll need to do something more proactive to get noticed. You have got to have your website optimized in order for it to show up in searches…and that's where SEO comes in. I'd say 75% of the new clients who come to me have no idea if their site is optimized or not, even if they had paid a webmaster to create it.

Another word of caution: SEO is a specialty and most webmasters are clueless about it. They design websites, don't optimize them, and their clients don't know to even ask. And then their clients wonder why they hardly get any traffic to their websites.

Other webmasters "claim" to know SEO and tell their clients they will design AND optimize the website. But the webmaster only knows the very basics of SEO and the client suffers because of it.

If you choose to hire a webmaster who claims to understand SEO, make sure to ask for client references and inquire about the traffic their website receives. Chances are they'll realize their site wasn't optimized very well either.

Whether you hire a webmaster or create a website yourself, my advice is to also hire an SEO specialist who can advise you, or work with your webmaster, to make sure your new website is optimized correctly.

Again, it's a total waste of your time and money to have a website created that no one can find when doing keyword searches on the Internet. And if a webmaster tells you they have set-up a Google™ Analytics account for you that does NOT mean your site has been optimized! It simply means you have a tool that will enable you to review your web traffic stats. But there won't be much to review if your site is not optimized!

Your Business Cards: Pay a designer to create a nice business card design for you with your new logo. It's not expensive. Then you can upload your design file to an online printing service like PrintingForLess.com. You can get 500 business cards, 4-color, 2-sides, on quality paper stock, for under $100. And they are delivered in less than 10 working days!

You'll want to have your cards with you at all times and have a good-sized stack with you when you go to networking events or speaking engagements. It's very embarrassing to have someone ask you for a business card and not be able to produce one…especially if he/she could be a potential client!

Your Word Templates & Marketing Materials: Create letterhead and proposal templates in Word with your logo and contact info on them. These will make you look very professional when you send documents to people who inquire about your services, pricing, speaking topics, etc. Most of my communications are electronic, so I didn't even bother to have my letterhead printed. I have a color laser printer that works just fine on the rare occasion I need to actually print out a letter or my marketing materials and *snail mail* them to someone. A majority of the time I convert my documents to PDF files and email them.

You can go to Acrobat.com to download inexpensive software that will easily convert your Word docs to PDF files. A PDF file protects your content so it can't be altered by the recipient, whereas anyone can edit a Word doc you send.

In terms of collateral material, I use my Word doc proposal template for multiple purposes. For example, my **Services Overview Package** outlines my package options, services, pricing, as well as client policies and procedures. It also includes my bio. My **Presentations Overview Package** outlines my speaking topics, pricing, speaking policies and procedures, along with my bio. I also have **Custom Proposals** that I use when I'm asked to provide a proposal for a specific project, sponsorship program or speaking engagement.

My Services Overview Package is given to potential *consulting & coaching clients*, and the Presentations Overview Package is for *speaking engagement inquiries.* They each serve a different purpose and go to different types of buyers. And, although a lot of the information in each one can be found on my website, negotiable details such as my policies and procedures and pricing are NOT available on my site(s). You have to contact me directly for that information. However, some topic experts do put their consulting and speaking fees on their websites. It's totally up to you!

Your Bookkeeping: I do not do my own bookkeeping. I'm not a CPA, I'm not a financial expert, and the only class I've taken on this subject was a semester of Accounting 101 in high school.

Over the years as a business owner, however, I've learned how to read financial reports and make educated decisions from that information. I just don't want to input the daily and weekly data that creates them.

Honestly, a lot of it makes my head spin so I let the experts handle it. My time is better spent on running my business and being creative, not spending hours each week doing bookkeeping...that I'd do incorrectly anyway.

When I owned my advertising agency, I had the same full-time Office Manager, Julie, who was with me for over 16 years. I love her like a sister! She is now a freelance bookkeeper who is a Certified ProAdvisor specializing in QuickBooks®, and she works with small business clients. Happily, I am one of them. I recommend that all of you find a "Julie" to help you get your books set-up correctly and help you maintain them.

Julie has told me that a vast majority of her initial time with new clients is spent cleaning up the mess they've made trying to do their own bookkeeping...even when they've been using a respected bookkeeping software program like QuickBooks. Just because you have the software doesn't mean you know how to use it correctly! And many small business owners get so busy running their companies they get really behind on their bookkeeping, and that is a serious trap you don't want to get caught in.

My belief is that there are many other places that are not as important as my financial books where I can try to save a buck, so why try to cut costs on my bookkeeping? And in the long run it also saves me money on tax prep because my CPA is given clean, organized books to work with at tax-time versus the big mess that I'd be sure to create.

Plus, Julie has my business set-up with QuickBooks Online so she and my CPA can access my books anytime, from anywhere, and so can I. It's a fabulous solution and one you should consider...as long as you also have a "Julie" to make sure it's set-up, utilized and maintained correctly!

Okay. That concludes Part One! So far we've discussed how you can turn what you know into dough, what to do to create your new (or improved) brand platform, and I've outlined the business and branding tools you need to get started. NOW it's time to start telling the world you exist so you can start generating revenue. So let's dive in to Part Two!

Promote U Thru
Powerful PR

"Don't believe that stuff about the world beating a path to the door of the person with a better mousetrap. The world, in fact, will beat a path to the person who sets out enough cheese...for the media."

~ Howard Bragman
CEO of the Public Relations Agency, Fifteen Minutes, Author of *Where's My Fifteen Minutes? Get Your Company, Your Cause, or Yourself the Recognition You Deserve*

INTRODUCTION TO PART TWO

Promote U Thru Powerful PR

I would say most every new client that comes to me has never written a press release and has never had any type of PR strategy to build awareness for their brand. This is a big boo-boo. (Ouch!) Why? Because PR can be inexpensive to implement, yet still get you massive exposure.

Whether you want to get local, national or global media exposure, it can happen. And a press release is the tool that can make it happen.

So in this section we're going to discuss how to write an effective press release and then where you can distribute it. We're also going to discuss strategies that you can utilize to contact the media and grab their attention.

Media such as the *The New York Times, Wall Street Journal,* ABC, MSNBC and NPR didn't interview me out of the goodness of their hearts and the desire to help me succeed. I courted them… I lured them…I engaged them. More importantly, I crafted press releases and did media outreach to get their attention. And once the doors opened, and I created relationships with journalists and producers from a wide variety of media, the interview requests kept coming…even when I *didn't* send out a release. This happy situation came to pass because they now perceive me as *an expert,* and when topics come up that they know I can comment on, they call me.

That is my goal for you. I want to get you positioned as a go-to expert so you can generate *massive* media coverage! If that's your goal, too, keep reading.

CHAPTER FIVE
Writing a Press Release That Rocks

By Lisa Orrell

After you have defined your brand positioning and created your basic branding and business tools (such as a website, business cards and collateral), it is important to focus on letting the mass market (or even your local area) know you exist. And one of the most effective tools you can use to accomplish this is a press release campaign.

Plus, press releases can benefit you in ways that that other marketing tools can't. The two main benefits of PR are *credibility and exposure*. You can tell everyone how great you are in your marketing materials, but being interviewed by, or mentioned in, a magazine, newspaper, radio or TV program, or popular blog or podcast, is a *third-party endorsement* that positions you as an "expert" in your niche. And this will not only attract clients and paid speaking opportunities to you, but can also provide you with exposure, quickly, to the audience you want to reach.

And PR can go beyond building your "expert" brand positioning. It's an effective tool for promoting events you're conducting (webinars, teleseminars, workshops and seminars) and announcing products you have created (books, e-books, videos, etc.).

By distributing press releases, I have been interviewed by tons of well-known major media, as well as regional and local media. And when you give them a great interview or sound bite, you have a good chance they'll come back to you. I know one freelance journalist, who writes for several national newspapers, that has interviewed me three different times in the past six months for different articles she was writing. That is FREE publicity for me that reaches around the world.

Press releases can also prompt the media to ask you to write articles for them. Why? They perceive you as an expert! In a short period of time I was asked by major print and online media to write articles for them—all because they received releases from me. Those releases put me on their radar as a go-to expert in my niche.

How to Write an Effective Press Release

If you've never written a press release before, you may find the process a little daunting. To make it easier for you, I'd like to provide you with some very helpful tips for not only crafting one, but also where to deploy it on online so that the media actually sees it…and so that it shows up in Google searches to provide on-going traffic to your website. And, remember, once it's deployed online, it will show up in search engine results forever. So, even when it becomes "old news," your press release(s) can continue to generate traffic to your website and build awareness for you.

Ready? Let's get started…

1. **Make Sure It's Newsworthy:** Some people want to write a press release about everything and anything they do, but that's not a good strategy. You should only send out a release when you have worthwhile news, such as: the release of a book, landing a significant speaking engagement, an event you're conducting, or a new product you've created. And never forget that press releases are not meant to be written like articles or ads—they are meant to be "news"!

2. **The Headline:** Make sure it's to the point, and not like the headline of an ad, eblast or direct mail piece. A press release is not a "marketing" promotional piece; it's meant to share news in a factual, straightforward way. Your headline should be 20 words or less and contain the main information of your story.

3. **The Body Copy:** I have read many press releases that read like an ad or marketing brochure. Wrong! Using hype, exclamation points, marketing speak, etc. is not appropriate and editors, reporters, etc. will ignore it.

4. **Basic Structure:** Headline; short sub-head (synopsis); main intro paragraph that covers the "5 W's" (who, what, where, when and why) because some media may only run your first paragraph and not the whole thing; second paragraph with more support info or a quote from you; a third paragraph with more support info and details about what you're announcing; a fourth paragraph with a quote/testimonial from a client or industry expert about you that relates to the news of your press release; a fifth paragraph with boilerplate info about your business; and a short final paragraph with your contact info. Keep the paragraphs short and try to keep the length to around 1-1.5 pages. You can find free press release examples online, so I recommend reviewing a few before you write yours. And PRWeb.com has a great tutorial for novice PR writers.

5. **Add Testimonials:** It's always good to include one testimonial so that someone else is quoted in it saying how amazing you are. It gives you more credibility. But, as mentioned in #4, make sure their quote relates to the news you are sharing. An alternative is to include data or statistical information from a respected third party to add substance.

6. **Get Client, Organization or Individual Approval:** If you want to mention a client, or any other organization, business, or person, in your release, get approval first! This is BIG. For example you may have just landed a keynote speech for a high profile organization and now want to tell the world about it. Yes, this type of news would be worthy of a press release, BUT the entity that hired you may have strict policies about being mentioned in *someone else's* story (mandated by their legal departments). And you can get into A LOT of trouble sending out a press release without their permission—A LOT of trouble (as in *sued*).

7. **Optimize Your Press Release for Online Search:** Add 5-10 keywords or phrases that have received good online search results because when you deploy your press release through an online service, those keywords will help it be found by people doing

searches related to the topic of your story. As of this writing, Google offers a free keyword search tool at:

https://adwords.google.com/select/KeywordToolExternal

You can type in keywords and phrases into this tool and it will tell you how many searches were done for them within specific timeframes. This will help you determine which ones are worth putting into your press release copy. The tool will also provide you with variations of the keywords you came up with that may yield even better results.

Note: When you find a few popular words and phrases don't repeat them a lot in the copy thinking it will improve your search results. Search engines only detect them once anyway. For example, if the tool reveals that "Business Coach for Small Business Owners" gets significant searches every month, you only need to work that phrase into your press release one time, not several.

Before we move onto the next chapter and the topic of press release distribution, I would like to mention something. If you're not a great writer, or you are struggling to come up with worthwhile angles for a press release, seek help. I realize you may be on a tight budget, so I'm not advocating getting into a monthly retainer with a PR Consultant. But it could be very worthwhile to hire a professional for just a few hours of consultation and brainstorming.

I recently had a one-hour consulting session with a client and I was able to develop five newsworthy press release ideas for her in that one session. This happens a lot in my client sessions. And, please note, a lot of my clients don't think they have anything newsworthy to write about. Or, the news they think is worthwhile isn't. Why is this? Because most of them don't have marketing backgrounds!

So getting an outside perspective from a professional can really be beneficial to your PR efforts…even if it's just a few hours, occasionally, of consultation time.

CHAPTER SIX

How to Distribute Your Press Release and Contact the Media

By Lisa Orrell

Great! Your press release is written. Now what? You'll want to deploy it through an online service. There are tons of free and paid distribution services out there, but be careful! Some of them are a total waste of time and money.

Here's a few that most PR experts I know use, and that I use (and recommend to clients):

1. PRWeb.com (to reach a U.S. audience)
2. BusinessWire.com
3. PR9.net
4. PRNewsWire.com (to reach an international audience)

These services vary in cost and offer several different package options that will allow you to: choose the industry(s), audience, and media you want to reach; add keywords; select the date of deployment; add pictures, images and logos to the upload; and view on-going traffic stats for your press release. Ultimately, you'll need to make decisions based on your budget.

PR9.net is very inexpensive—around $15 (US) per press release upload. Even when I use one of the other more expensive services listed above, I always deploy through PR9.net, too. I do this because I find my press releases deployed through this service show-up in Google searches, and that's worth $15 to me. They don't offer all the bells and whistles the other services do, but they do allow you to add keywords and choose industry categories.

Also, in addition to deploying your release online for mass coverage and distribution, you'll want to create a **targeted, specific**

list of media you want to reach. Then you can email your press release directly to them and do follow-up calls and correspondence.

Why create a media list even when you deploy your press release online? Because you are not guaranteed the specific media you want to see it *actually will see it*. Deploying online distributes it to the *masses*, but there will also be local media, or specific blogs, magazines, broadcast media or online media, that are perfect for your topic. So you want to make sure they receive it, too, and the only way to ensure the media you consider your 'A List' is in the loop is to contact them directly.

Important Note: Don't attach the press release to your email! Because of problems with viruses, many media outlets simply don't open attachments. Instead, cut and paste the press release text into the body of your email.

Spoon-Feeding the Media Segment Ideas

In addition to sending out "mass news" press releases, there is another strategy for getting publicity. I call it "spoon-feeding" the media. The media loves it when you approach them with *specific* story ideas. This can be along the lines of topics like: "Is Your Career Suffering? 5 Unique Tips for Success" or "Do You Struggle With Money? 3 Surefire Tips for Finding Financial Bliss" or "Is Stress Ruining Your Life? 4 Proven Ways to Overcome It."

The key here is you're doing the "thinking" for the reporters, editors, TV segment producers, etc. These people are always looking for ideas, and appreciate when they get them! So focus on topics that fit within your expertise, develop compelling topics that would be great interview topics for print, online, radio or TV, find several media outlets that cover stories related to your expertise and that *reach your target audience*, and then pitch them your idea(s). This strategy has worked very well for me, personally, and for my clients, too!

You can approach the media contacts via phone or email. But, and here's a key point: whether you send them a press release or contact them with a specific story idea, you need to follow-up.

Sending media people one email or leaving one voicemail message is typically not enough. Try **3-5 follow up attempts** before you give up. Most members of the media are approached with a flood of news stories and topic ideas daily, so being the squeaky wheel is often necessary. And even if they don't jump on the first idea you present, continue to the send them new ones. Eventually you will get their attention!

Please keep this in mind: We live in a 24/7, 365 days per year, media society. Round-the-clock cable networks, major networks, radio networks, print media networks, and online media, have a TON of time and space they need to fill. So they are always looking for interesting story angles, and experts to interview...*and you can be one of them!*

Sharing Your News Thru Social Media

Once you have written a press release, be sure to post it on your website (on your Media or News page), and share the link with all of your Social Media channels: Facebook, Twitter, LinkedIn, MySpace, etc. You can also re-purpose the press release as a post for your blog.

And, when you start to get media interviews, be sure to put links to the articles or media appearances on your website. Plus, share links to those, too, with your Social Media communities. Please note, it's not only totally acceptable to toot your own horn by sharing these things, it is necessary!

OKAY! There is your crash course in how implementing effective PR strategies can benefit your business. Again, this is a key marketing tool for building brand awareness, positioning yourself as an expert, generating sales for events and products, and attracting new clients to your business.

Being *persistent and consistent* with your PR efforts can bring you substantial returns...and prospects will be impressed by the media coverage you post on your website. It really will build your credibility as a leading expert, or business, in your industry!

Promote U Thru
Solid Social Media Strategies

"Social Media isn't the end-all-be-all, but it offers marketers unparalleled opportunity to participate in relevant ways. It also provides a launch pad for other marketing tactics. Social Media is not an island. It's a high-power engine on the larger marketing ship."

~ Matt Dickman, *technomarketer.typepad.com*

"Quit counting fans, followers and blog subscribers like bottle caps. Think, instead, about what you're hoping to achieve with and through the community that actually cares about what you're doing."

~ Amber Naslund, *Social Media Today*

INTRODUCTION TO PART THREE

Promote U Thru Solid Social Media Strategies

You are going to learn a ton in this section! Why? Because, I reached out to colleagues who are truly experts in the specific areas we'll be covering, and they graciously contributed chapters loaded with great tips. There's no way you won't get loads of useful strategies from these specialists who are highly respected in the world of Social Media.

This is "required reading" for anyone who wants to position themselves as an expert in today's marketplace...so take notes! Every day I work with clients who have no idea what to do with different Social Media tools and how to use it to move forward professionally. Sure, they know what they are, but they ask me things like: *I want to start a blog, but what would I write about?* Or, *If I get on Twitter or start a Fan Page, what would I do?* Or, *I have a Fan Page, but what should I be doing with it?* Or, *What kinds of things should I post on YouTube?* Or, *I'm on LinkedIn, but what should I be doing there?* And on and on and on...

I also understand that some of you may be past those questions, and well on your way using Social Media effectively. But don't skip this section! You are bound to learn some new tips and emerging strategies that can improve your current efforts.

Here's a snapshot of the experts who will be your "teachers" in this section, adding their thoughts to mine: Jessica Northey, SocialMediologist; Eve Mayer Orsburn, CEO of Social Media Delivered; Mirna Bard, Founder of NuReach Global; Lynn Baldwin-Rhoades, Founder of both Marketing Shebang & Power Chicks International; David Steel, President of The Steel Method; Bill Graham-Reefer, President of WorldView PR; and Susan Young, President of Get in Front Communications, Inc.

Okay, without further delay…(drum roll, please)…are you ready to get the scoop on how to effectively use Facebook, Twitter, LinkedIn, YouTube and Blogs to build your brand and increase your business? Great!

It's going to be a wild Social Media education ride, so jump in, buckle up, and hold on!

CHAPTER SEVEN

Avoid Suffering From Social "Me"dia Syndrome: A Deadly Epidemic That Can Kill Your Brand-Building and Business Growth

By Lisa Orrell

Could you be suffering from Social "Me"dia Syndrome and not even know it? Unfortunately, this common ailment is causing millions of businesses and individuals serious pain when it comes to their online brand-building and business growth efforts.

What is *Social "Me"dia Syndrome?* It's when people make these three common mistakes:

- They take the "Social" out of Social Media

- They spend too much time focused on the "Me" in Media

- They don't spend enough time participating in their online communities (such as Twitter, Facebook, LinkedIn, and blogs)

How much time do people spend on Social Media activities? A recent report conducted and published by Michael A. Stelzner, Founder of SocialMediaExaminer.com entitled "2010 Social Media Marketing Industry Report: How Marketers Are Using Social Media to Grow Their Business" shared that *people who are just getting started using Social Media only commit about one hour per week to their efforts.* And that time frame is the average that I hear when I talk to people who are struggling with their Social Media programs. But <u>one hour per week</u> is just not enough time to get decent results!

So how much time *should* be allocated? Personally, I spend **6-12 hours per week** on my Social Media channels. And, in a fairly short period of time, this has generated clients, media interviews, and terrific strategic partnerships for me.

The Stelzner report supports that average time commitment, stating: *6+ hours per week was common among people who had been using Social Media for brand and business growth for several months or more*, and a *significant 85% of all marketers indicated that their Social Media efforts have generated exposure for their businesses.* The lesson here? If you're not getting results, but are only spending a few hours per week committed to your efforts, you may be getting back exactly what you are putting in.

There's No 'I' in Social Media

But what about the other two common mistakes mentioned earlier: Taking the word "Social" out of Social Media and spending too much time focused on the "Me" in Media? The answer is quite simple: If you get involved in Social Media, but make it all about you, you'll suffer. Many people simply don't participate in their online communities, or just post and tweet self-focused content and comments. These are big problems I see a lot.

People typically follow others on Twitter, "like" their Fan Page, and/or read their blog to learn from that person's expertise. They don't log on to Facebook or Twitter to constantly get pitch messages asking them to attend events, buy products, hire services, etc. But, unfortunately, many people use their Social Media channels to do nothing more than sell, sell, sell.

Could *you* be suffering from Social "Me"dia Syndrome? Review these 10 questions to find out:

1. If you have a blog, do you **follow other peoples' blogs and post interesting comments**? Or do you simply expect people to follow your blog?

2. Do you really **participate in the Facebook Fan Pages or Groups you've joined**? Or do you expect everyone just to flock to yours?

3. Do you **answer questions or provide solutions** to people you follow on Twitter?

4. Do you **re-tweet the tweets of others**?

5. Do you **thank people for re-tweeting** you or following you?

6. Do you take the time to **participate in things like #FollowFriday #FF on Twitter** and recommend tweeps you really like so your followers will then know about them, too?

7. If you have a Facebook Fan Page, **do you actually go there, regularly**, and post questions or helpful info that your Fans can respond to or benefit from?

8. If you have a blog, do you invite **Guest Bloggers** to write posts and then source them clearly?

9. Do you reach out to people on LinkedIn, participate in Group Discussions, and **offer advice when questions are asked?**

10. On your Facebook Fan Page, do you **post interesting questions** on the Discussion Board, let your Fans know, encourage them to answer the questions, and/or post new questions?

If you answered "No" to more than 3 of these questions, you have Social "Me"dia Syndrome. And this means your branding, marketing, partnering, sales, and lead generation efforts, will be or are, suffering.

The cure? Take 2 aspirin, shift your perspective, reassess your goals and efforts, and jump in more consistently...*and selflessly!* Chances are, within a short period of time, you'll be feeling much better about the results you get through Social Media...and you'll be cured!

CHAPTER EIGHT

Making Social Media Work for You and Your Brand

By Jessica Northey

"The right message, to the right people, the right amount of times."

This is the *"Holy Trinity"* of advertising: getting the message you want created, transmitted to the ideal audience, and having it hit right when you want it to.

You can have a great commercial, *but buy a very small schedule.* Or you can put a commercial that speaks to women fifty plus *on an alternative rock station.* Both are examples of how the greatest message in the world doesn't matter if you're not reaching the *right audience,* or not reaching your audience frequently enough. It is easy to see how the same rules can apply to Social Media marketing efforts. Understanding how your target audience (as defined by gender, age, and geography) uses Social Media will determine your goals and strategy.

So, what *is* the 'right' message? And who are the 'right' people? And what exactly is the 'right' number of times to deploy that message?

Part I: The Right Message

Are you trying to attract tweens looking for a cell phone or mature females who want a manicure?

Before you begin the process or even if you have already started and feel lost, worry about Social Media tools/platforms last, not first. *The tools will always change.* AOL once ruled the Cybersphere with chat rooms and just a short time ago I had to check MySpace 10 or 15 times a day because I was addicted to it. So if you get hung up on tools, you'll constantly be changing directions.

A solid Social Media marketing plan should include details about your business's unique selling points, pricing strategy, your sales and distribution plan, and your plans for advertising and promotions.

Put goals in writing. Written goals equal success! "We have got to get on Twitter, Facebook and Blog" is not a goal or strategy; it is just a statement. So define what you want to accomplish. What is your purpose? In addition, when you define your goals, you manage your own expectations! You can also use analytical tools, demographics and psychographics to determine how to segment the market you are trying to reach.

Ask yourself:
• Can you describe what your company does in 140 characters or less?
• What is the point of your message?
• What type of client are you talking for? Potential or Existing?
• What is your Relationship with client or potential client?
• How will you humanize your company?
• How can you use influence lines instead of sell lines?

Social Media is most unique and useful for delivering the right message because you control the message and can respond quickly and appropriately to any issue. I can send out a press release, but when it is transformed to news, what a journalist does with it can easily change *my* story. With Social Media, I get my thoughts, news and comments out the way I want.

Just exactly how do you find your own voice online and figure out what to say? In other words, what is your Social*ality*? Just like your personality, your Social*ality* should reflect you or your brand's unique attributes including behavioral, temperamental, emotional and mental aspects that give you character! The most beneficial use of Social Media is to present the combination of all the quirks and different things that give you or the people who work at your company **character**.

Picture this: you are at a networking event talking to someone and they mention that there is going to be great weather for the NASCAR race this weekend. A few things could happen...your eyes might glaze over and you hear something that sounds like the teachers voice on Charlie Brown "waah wah wah, wah wah wah waah" or if you were to meet me, you would soon find out that I am a huge Motorhead!

Then the next person you talk to mentions that she used to work at her college radio station. You relate to this because you used to work as an on-air radio personality before getting into outside media sales.

The person after that breeds Pomeranian-Chihuahuas. And then the next person drinks the same brand of wine as you.

The point is we naturally filter the noise of our personalities with each other and find people we have common ground with.

Social Media does the same, and the interaction on sites like Twitter, Facebook, and LinkedIn is meant to be social (a friendly gathering). Also realize that you can be personable without being too personal. Give a little of yourself...listen to what others say about themselves and then find out where similar interests lie. This is how you can build relationships!

Just to reiterate: Social Media is an umbrella term that describes websites that connect individuals in some way. And an indicating quality of Social Media is the user generated content. User-generated content comes from your experience, strengths and hopes, and let's your audience know who you are.

Part II: The Right People
Do you want to talk to golfers in Tucson or hunters in Wisconsin?

You know your business better than anyone else. And by the time you take your marketing efforts "Web 2.0" you should have identified your target audience. Generally this is done as part of your business plan design. You know what kind of service or product you sell, and who you want to buy them.

Your choices about what Social Media platform to participate in should logically reflect where your customers and prospective customers are and how you want to interact with them. You can determine demographic, psychographic and lifestyle data to determine what your customers' interests are. You can target and follow other company's like yours, or even follow and monitor your competitors' Social Media usage.

Here's how I characterize the various (current) Social Media networking sites:
- LinkedIn: Work or industry event you have been invited to.
- Facebook Personal Profile: Backyard BBQ.
- MySpace: Going clubbing with the friends.
- Blogging: Coffee shop talk.
- Twitter: Happy Hour Networking Event Mixer.

Okay. You know *who* you want, now *how* do you find them?

Facebook, LinkedIn, your website, and your blog are all limited to the people you bring to them, so it can be difficult to grow outside your existing network. This is why Twitter is such a great tool to increase traffic to other Social Media platforms including your blog, YouTube, Facebook Fan Page, MySpace or even LinkedIn. I even have clients who report increases of website traffic up to 5000% through Twitter efforts.

So, you are on Twitter, but how do you find the right people? Sifting through the overwhelming volume of content and services in order to connect with people you want to find can be overwhelming and frustrating. At the time of this writing, there are many tools and ways to find followers.

This is what I did and recommend you do:

- **Sign up for the Twitter Directories** http://wefollow.com/ and http://www.Twellow.com. Wefollow.com is a user-powered Twitter directory organized by interests that helps you find Twitter celebrities, actors, TV personalities, or new Twitter friends in your area. And Twellow.com is a directory of public

Twitter accounts, with hundreds of categories and search features to help you find people who matter to you.

- **Find people to Tweet with** at http://search.twitter.com. Twitter itself has expanded its suggested users into about 20 categories and made those suggestions available to all users, not just new signups as well.

You can search to find people that you have things in common with; you will want to follow the people who are following them. These are people you have something in common with and they will most likely follow you back.

You can use the advanced feature to locate people of like interest and find out what people are saying about you, your brand, your industry, etc. Both services are free and great for SEO and indexing, as well as finding other Twitterers looking for you or your service. And they help you "cut through the clutter."

Next Question: What does your potential consumer know about you right now?

It's too confusing to have a single strategy that targets advocates AND people that have never heard of you. That should be two strategies. You need to hold a mirror up to your target consumer and use words, phrases, suggestions that appeal to them. You need to really understand how your target consumer (as defined by gender, age, and geography) uses Social Media. If your audience skews older, you probably will not want to engage in a lot of "make a video" contests since that target audience indexes low on the "Create Media" scale.

Part III: The Right Amount of Time
How often should you tweet, post or blog?

This is going to be different for everyone. You know your clients and potential client's best. As we mentioned in "The Right People," you will need to determine who they are. Pinpoint the characteristics of the perfect customer as it relates to your product or service. Understand how your target audience uses Social Media and then be there when they are there. Here are some key tips:

• Listen and then listen more.

• Ask yourself the following questions when you are designing Social Media optimization campaigns: What's your point? What type of program is this? What is your purpose? Awareness, Sales, Loyalty? What's your relationship with audience? What does your audience know about you today? When and where is your audience using Social Media?

• Who are you to this audience?

• Elevator pitch or 60 second commercials are obsolete how do you describe who you are or what you do in 140 characters or less?

The other day a friend of mine in the entertainment industry asked me to follow them on Twitter. Curious, I took a peek at their Twitter profile info. At first glance, I noticed this person was only following a handful of people and then, that they were only broadcasting information about what they were doing AND what they had to say. No interaction with others…just a laundry list all about THEM, with no real purpose. That really turned me off and I didn't actually follow them. I figured this person wouldn't notice anyways, since they had hundreds of followers. However knowing this person, I couldn't help but think if they would follow people and engage them, they would probably have thousands of followers.

My philosophy is to follow everyone back, for a couple reasons:

• I don't think I am better than anyone else. I can't even begin to understand why it is so important to have people following you that you aren't following.

• You never know where your next friend or lead is going to come from. Guy Kawasaki, early-Twitter adopter and world-renowned marketing expert with one of the largest Twitter followings on that social network explained, "When I first started on Twitter, Robert Scoble told me to follow everyone who followed me. But why, I asked him, would I follow everyone like that? Robert explained it's the courteous thing to do and because when you do, some people will respond to you and everyone who follows them will see this— which is more exposure for you."

Most people are used to **broad***casting* or even *narrow***casting**. *So, let me introduce you to your new best friend:* **Communicasting!**

Communicasting is the exchange of thoughts, messages or ideas, by transferring information from one to another, or many to each other and connecting with other people. We all could do better by thinking a little less about ourselves and more about others.

How do you connect with others? I suggest:

• Speak with people, not at them!

• Ask *them* questions.

• Check out *their* profiles.

• Ask them about their town, career, children, animals, family.

• Check out the link to their websites.

• Read their blogs…and post comments

• Notice their photos or background.

• Forget, 'What am I doing?' and ask your followers, 'What are YOU doing?'

I am often asked, "How did you get so many followers?" Honestly it has nothing to do with rocket science, it is completely human science…I followed people who followed me and I followed people I thought were interesting.

Try to remember that you have to learn how to give a little to get a little.

About the Author: With over 20 years of media experience including television, radio, Internet, and print sales, as well as being an on-air personality, Jessica Northey is known for the ability to create compelling marketing campaigns and bridge partnerships. Jessica is the Associate Editor and Social Media Expert for FullThrottleCountry.com, Country Music Radio's interactive idea-sharing new media platform. And, in her weekly column, "Finger Candy Friday," Jessica gives advice and opinions about Social Media trends and topics. Plus, as the founder of Finger Candy Media, LLC, Jessica helps Celebrities, Musicians, Brands and Businesses use Social Media strategically to accomplish their productivity goals.

Contact Info:
Jessica Northey
SocialMediologist
Jessicanorthey@gmail.com
http://fingercandymedia.com/
1-559-349-5933
Twitter @JessicaNorthey
Fan Page: Facebook.com/FingerCandyMedia
LinkedIn: Jessica Northey

CHAPTER NINE

LINKEDIN: Leveraging the Most Affluent Social Media Network To Grow Your Business

By Eve Mayer Orsburn

In this book, you are lucky to be hearing from experts about all different types of Social Media platforms, such as Facebook and Twitter, which have hundreds of millions of users. So, why would a social network like LinkedIn, which is a fraction of the size (at a mere 75 millions members at the time I am typing this), be worthy of an entire chapter? Well, my friend, let me open your eyes, and, hopefully, fatten your wallets with all the ways you can wield this Social Media tool.

Facebook is like a public party, Twitter is like an office party, and LinkedIn is like a **professional networking event.**

Now, before you freak out, calm down. I also use both Facebook and Twitter—in fact, on Twitter, I am known as @LinkedInQueen. But, I understand how each of these Social Media tools should be used, who I can reach with them, and what I can accomplish. So should you by the way, so make sure to read every chapter of this book!

So, why LinkedIn? Why do you keep on getting those invites to join someone on LinkedIn? It is because LinkedIn is currently **the largest professional social network**, meaning the entire purpose of LinkedIn is to get business done. It's not the place to talk about your cat, post pictures of your son, or share your favorite recipes (unless you are a professional chef). And amazingly, most people on LinkedIn stick to talking business. For those of you out there who still think Social Media is a waste of time, perhaps LinkedIn might be the perfect place for you to start and become a convert and fall deeply, deeply in love with Social Media. That's what happened to me!

Many years ago, I signed up for LinkedIn, filled out a few lines of my profile in about 5 minutes, and never gave it another thought. I wasn't on Facebook, I wasn't on Twitter—seriously, who had the time and how would any of those things add something to my life?

Then, a few years ago, I went back to LinkedIn and took a second look. It was around the same time that the economy had taken a nose dive and everyone was scared—including me. People were not calling me back, prospects were not answering their emails, and I needed a new way to find business. This need brought me to LinkedIn, and there I found the right people to talk to…and I found leads. Did LinkedIn magically solve the recession? No! But it did afford me a new and efficient way of researching, partnering, learning, interacting, prospecting, and representing myself. And when times get tough, business owners better get tougher and faster. That is what LinkedIn afforded me the ability to do.

LinkedIn is also the most affluent Social Media network today, with an average member household income around $108,000 (at the time I am writing this) according to LinkedIn. Every Fortune 500 company is represented on LinkedIn, and the last time I checked, the average user age was higher than Facebook and Twitter users. What does this all mean? If you are interested in finding a job, getting funding for your startup, finding strategic partners for your business, or researching your competitors, chances are LinkedIn is the right place to make it happen.

How to Begin on LinkedIn:

Maybe you are already on LinkedIn, and you are thinking this woman has got to be kidding me. Perhaps you filled in your LinkedIn profile years ago, and you even took time to fill it out almost completely. But, you have never, ever gotten one job, one partner, or one prospect from LinkedIn. This means two things: a.) you are like most people, and b.) you are not leveraging the tool anywhere close to its capacity.

The first step to unlocking the power of LinkedIn is to set up your profile completely and effectively. Treat this like getting dressed up for a networking event that is going to be full of the professionals you need to reach. Your LinkedIn profile is your "outfit," and when people meet you virtually on LinkedIn, they will make judgments and decisions based on your 'appearance' just like they do in real life. They will want to know right away who you are, why you are important, and most of all—what you can do for them. So, put that information succinctly into your profile with your name, heading and summary.

The next step in using LinkedIn is to import your contacts. LinkedIn makes it very easy for you to import your contacts and then choose who you want to send invitations to so they will connect with you. LinkedIn will also tell you which of your contacts are already on LinkedIn, and these are the only people I think you should send your invitation request out to right away. Many people only import their professional contacts, but I think the best idea is to import all of your contacts, *including business and personal,* into LinkedIn. After all, haven't you ever gotten a job, business deal or lead from a friend or neighbor? Big business can typically come from *personal* connections, so use them here!

Once you are connected to people on LinkedIn, there is an easy way to stay in front of them. Update your LinkedIn status (the little white box below your headline), location, and industry at the top of your profile. You should treat these 140 characters like your own personal billboard, where you highlight the most interesting thing you are working on that day. This information will populate onto the home pages of your connections, which will keep you in top of mind awareness.

When you reach out to new people on LinkedIn in the correct way, the first thing they are going to do is click your profile, view your picture, quickly scan your summary, and decide if they will respond. If your profile is done well, you'll get many more responses than you would typically get from just sending a regular email. An email does not usually come with a picture, a bio-like summary, and a mini history of your professional career at the recipient's disposal to peruse. LinkedIn puts all of this information within reach with just a click.

LinkedIn looks pretty simple when you first use it, but you'll be amazed at how extensive and huge the network actually is. I can spend hours on LinkedIn, and sometimes have a hard time stopping. The information I can find on the site is so valuable, it's hard to walk away. Some of my favorite areas of LinkedIn are Advanced People Search, Groups, and Events, but there are plenty more areas that bring exciting and useful possibilities. Answers, Network Statistics, and polls are just a few of the tools you can utilize.

Most professionals can get just about everything they need from the free, basic version of LinkedIn. Some people who have a big daily need for searches and reach outs on LinkedIn should consider upgrading to the paid version. Sometimes there are exceptions, such as recruiters can benefit from the upgraded version because of a recruiter's rapid need to find candidates and contact them directly.

When you need to get something done in business, you think of the people who can help you achieve that goal. Sometimes, though, you don't have the right connections. And sometimes, you *do* have the right connections, but you don't even realize it! LinkedIn builds an instant roadmap showing you how you're connected to other people. You might not even realize that your neighbor from two houses down works at that company you've been hoping to partner with. But if you've imported your old neighbor into LinkedIn, and you search for the company you're interested in, the connection you never knew you had will appear right on the screen so you can take action.

There are now over 675,000 groups, covering just about every subject on LinkedIn, and you can join up to 50 of them. Here is your opportunity to meet people that you didn't even know before. Just remember, when you start joining groups, it is ok to join some that hold people that are like you and can teach you about your business and your industry, and form partnerships with you. However, if you are using LinkedIn as you should be, it is important to remember that you need be joining groups full of people very different from you that will help you reach your goals. For example, if you are a business owner who needs funding, join groups full of venture capitalist and angel investors. If you are a marketing executive for a medical device company, join groups full of medical professionals and doctors.

Once you are in a LinkedIn group, you will find discussions, news, jobs and information you cannot find anywhere else. Plus, you can post in these groups, including jobs, for free!

There are loads more things to explore on LinkedIn, but this should give you an excellent start. As with any Social Media, always remember that success starts with you connecting with others, assisting them, and sharing valuable information. If you still need help, make sure to connect with me. I'm probably on LinkedIn right now.

About the Author: Eve Mayer Orsburn is the CEO of Social Media Delivered and the author of *Social Media for the CEO: The Why and ROI of Social Media for the CEO of Today and Tomorrow.* Eve's background in business and traditional marketing lead her down a path of Social Media that began with Linkedin where she built her personal brand that developed into a worldwide brand. Eve is known by many as the LinkedinQueen. Her 40,000 connections online come from small businesses to Fortune 500 companies all looking to Eve for Social Media knowledge for business that they can actually understand. She speaks and consults on Social Media including Twitter, Facebook, YouTube, Blogs and more but admits that her favorite vehicle is Linkedin because of the power it brings in building business with the right people.

Contact Info:
Eve Mayer Orsburn
www.SocialMediaDelivered.com
www.Twitter.com/LinkedinQueen
www.Linkedin.com/in/EveMayerOrsburn

LISA ORRELL

CHAPTER TEN

TWITTER: 25 Surefire Ways to Engage and Influence People on Twitter

By Mirna Bard

It's no secret that Twitter is known as a "cocktail party on steroids," and the most talked about micro-blogging sensation on the Internet these days. World politicians, royalty, celebrities, athletes, global brands, the media, not-for-profits, and small businesses are all actively engaging in this rapidly-growing platform. They use it to stay connected to the world in real-time, gather instant feedback, and share information while observing a 140-character limit.

There truly has not been a medium out there that can benefit businesses and individuals as fast as Twitter, making it the darling of the Social Media world. Many businesses across the world are using this effective communication tool to monitor what their competition is doing and what their audience is saying, to build brand recognition and loyalty, to expand their communities, and to converse authentically with their target audience as well as create, discover and share ideas with others.

Thousands of companies have hopped onto the powerful Twitter bandwagon, trying to find a way to increase revenue one tweet at a time. **Comcast, Zappos,** and **Jet Blue** are now using Twitter to respond to customer queries. **Dell** and **Starbucks** use it to update customers on deals. **Whole Foods** and **Ford** use it to post company news and build stronger bonds with customers. A small business, **Kogi Korean BBQ Truck** in Los Angeles uses it to report the current location of the truck. Another small business, **Coffee Groundz**, uses the tool to expand their customer base by taking orders through Twitter as well as hosting tweet-ups at their location in Texas.

These examples are only a small sampling of how companies, big or small, have used Twitter to nurture customer relationships and expand their bottom line. And as tweeting becomes more popular, many companies feel extra pressure to join the social networking site in order to stay competitive.

Although the tool is very simple to use, it isn't as easy to Twitter—especially for businesses—as one might think. Many businesses still struggle to understand the Twitter culture, or neglect to put a great effort into leveraging this often-confusing platform. This struggle is not surprising since Twitter only debuted at the South by Southwest Tech Conference in April 2007. It is still a relatively new concept and understanding the ins and outs may not come as second nature to many people.

To assist you in leveraging your time on Twitter, I've compiled 25 surefire ways to engage and influence people on this popular social networking platform. Apply all these powerful tips and Twitter will become an irreplaceable asset to your Social Media plan. Twitter offers an exciting way to create openness, be authentic and "human," increase trust, improve expert status, gain loyal customers, and ultimately boost profitability. However, if you choose to ignore this practical advice, Twitter will be an awful time-suck without any benefits.

1. **Upload an avatar.** You should be using your own image on Twitter, not your pet, child, celebrity or logo. People want to create a relationship and do business with *you*, not an object.

2. **Be positive.** People shy away from the negative, so stay upbeat and you'll find more are drawn to you. Also, you'll receive more positive tweets, which is a definite plus.

3. **Earn the right.** Being interesting and amusing on Twitter, keeps followers loyal and makes you tweet-worthy. You should earn the right to attract followers, not have a Twitter stream that looks like a lifeless feed.

4. **Offer valuable information.** Giving useful tidbits will help you

attract followers, which will result in more retweets. Think about what would be the most helpful and valuable information to your followers.

5. **Comment on interesting tweets.** When you see an interesting tweet, reply back and comment on it. This is the most effective way to spark interactivity and get someone's attention.

6. **Be strategic.** Create strategic tweets, and don't say anything you don't want your great, great grandchildren to see, because tweets don't "go away." And remember, you only have 140 characters to get your point across and stand above all the chatter.

7. **Stay firm.** No one likes someone who wobbles between two opposing views, so don't be afraid to state your opinion on a topic. It might not be popular with everyone, but you'll gain respect for taking a stand.

8. **Avoid public arguments.** If you're going to be talking heatedly, keep it private with emails or direct messages (DM). There is no need to share with the world!

9. **Know when to DM.** Using the @reply on Twitter will still appear publicly, but a direct message will only be seen by that person. It's best to DM any confidential information (email addresses, etc.).

10. **Keep track of information.** Is one of your Twitter contacts pregnant? Make note of her due date and check in once in a while. People love it when others remember things that are important to them.

11. **Be a giver.** If someone is having a problem and you have a solution, let them know. If you can't help, retweet the message so someone else can help.

12. **Be funny.** Who doesn't love humor? Just be careful, humor doesn't always translate well over the Internet.

13. **Stay active.** Make sure you are tweeting on a daily basis. Most people will ignore someone who only pops up once in a while.

14. **Schedule your tweets.** If you're going to be offline for a while, make sure to use a system like Socialoomph to schedule some tweets, so it doesn't look like you have completely disappeared.

15. **Don't sell all the time**. You should always think relationships first, business second. A good rule of thumb is to have <u>two promotional tweets for every 10 content tweets</u>—apply the 80/20 rule.

16. **Promote others.** It is essential to promote others, and not just yourself. If you share other's great content and praise them for it, it is a win-win-win for you, the creator, and your followers.

17. **Respond quickly.** If you typically respond to someone more than 12 hours after they tweeted or asked you questions, chances are you don't have a good conversation going. Followers always appreciate a quick reply.

18. **Ask questions.** You'd be surprised how many people feel the need to answer a question and this is a great way to get the some fun conversations going.

19. **Get efficient.** There are many tools out there that help you be more efficient on Twitter. These tools are easier than logging on to Twitter—TweetDeck, Seesmic, and Hootsuite.

20. **Work on spelling.** Since most words are abbreviated, many people have atrocious spelling, which turns others off. You don't have to use a spellchecker, but learn the difference between lose and loose, at least.

21. **Retweet value.** Any time someone tweets something useful or worth sharing, make sure you retweet it. The original sender will appreciate this and so will your followers.

22. **Be human.** People will be more likely to chat with you if you are personable. That doesn't mean tweet about every detail of your life and juicy secrets, but showing followers that you're "human" is extremely effective.

23. **Share successes.** It is good to talk about your successes... without doing it in a gloating manner, of course. This often brings plenty of cheer from fellow tweeps and opens up the dialogue.

24. **Appreciate your followers.** Follow Friday is one meme that you can use, but simply thanking your new followers is a great way to go, or showing appreciation for retweets definitely goes a long way.

25. **Stop worrying.** Don't worry if competitors or copy-cats follow you. Here is your chance to differentiate yourself and prove that you have confidence your business is unique. You also never know what may result in joint-venture partnerships.

If you're a business owner who is still cautious of building your brand through Twitter, don't be. If your audience is on Twitter, then there is no doubt that you should be, too. To create a social presence and be found on Twitter, you must have a perpetual and consistent approach to listen, learn, communicate, measure, and repeat.

The bottom line is, if you're not participating in the online conversation, know that your competition is and they will get ahead in many ways. So, start to proactively brainstorm, carefully lay out your strategy, apply all 25 tips above, connect with your customers, and join in on the excitement because the digital world can be a great place to be!

Twitter Lingo
Many Twitter terms are foreign to many. Here are explanations of the most common terms to help you save time with Twitter:

Following: You can follow your target audience or people you're interested in. This means you see their updates in you're the stream or timeline of your home page. Equally, people get your messages by following you.

Tweeps or Tweeple: Users of Twitter are referred to as tweeps or tweeple.

Tweet: An individual message is referred to as a tweet. Tweets are public and need to be no more than 140 characters, including spaces and usernames.

@replies: If you want to talk directly to someone at Twitter or mention their username (aka handle), start with @<their Twitter name>. These messages will appear in search results and you can also track your own replies in the "@Replies" link on your Twitter page.

DM: This stands for direct message and is a way to send a private tweet. If you DM someone, you send the message directly to them and no one else can see it. To send one, start with the letter D (space) <person's Twitter name> or use the "Direct Messages" tab on profile page). *Note: You can only send DMs to the people who are following you.*

RT: Stands for "retweet" and means that the tweet is being reposted from someone else that found it interesting or helpful and wanted to share it with their followers. To retweet, start with RT @<their Twitter name> or click the retweet link on the bottom right as you hover each tweet.

Hashtags (#): These are used to keep track of tweets that are all part of a single subject, event, or topic. Use the pound sign (#) and any word relevant to the topic or event to create a hashtag.

Favorites: If you "favorite" a tweet, it means you want to save it for future reference. You can do this by clicking on the faded star to the right of each tweet, and you can see the "favorites" link listed on your profile page. Note: Others can see your favorites as well.

Trending Topics: On the right side of your screen and on the Twitter search page, you'll notice some trending topics, which are the hottest worldwide topics on Twitter at that moment. However, you can also narrow it down to your country or major cities.

Tweetup: An in-person gathering organized through Twitter. People use them for hosting launch parties and events, connecting with customers and introducing like-minded followers to each other.

About the Author: Named as one of the "smartest people in Social Media" and "top people to follow on Twitter" by various bloggers, Mirna Bard is a world-renowned business strategy expert, social web consultant for today's innovators, author and keynote speaker as well as instructor of Social Media strategy at the University of California, Irvine. Due to her expertise, she has been interviewed or quoted on websites/blogs and eBooks across the web as well as various media, including Orange County Register, Chief Executive Magazine, San Diego Living, Entrepreneur.com and many more.

Contact Info:
Mirna Bard
www.MirnaBard.com

CHAPTER ELEVEN

FACEBOOK: 7 Ways to Use the Power of Facebook for Business

By Lynn Baldwin-Rhoades

If your ideal client were just outside your office or store door, would you open it? What if you peeked out and saw not one person but five? How about 500 or even 5,000?

I imagine you'd throw open the door and happily greet them. You might start with a moment of small talk or ask how you could help them. Perhaps you'd offer a freebie or some information that would pique their interest in your product or service.

All the while, your stomach would be cart-wheeling as you marveled, *Where did these people come from, anyway? Did I just win the "ideal client" lottery?*

Welcome to Facebook—a lottery-like place where heaps of your perfect people are hanging out waiting for *you* to connect with them.

The Reality of Facebook Marketing

As a small business owner, entrepreneur or solopreneur, are you opening the door to this opportunity? Have you dipped into Facebook by creating a page (the way Facebookers "greet" one another) but left it to languish? Or are you saying, "Harrumph. Facebook's a fad. Why bother getting involved?"

The reality is, Facebook and other social networking tools have shaken up marketing much like Henry Ford's Model T shook up transportation back in the day. Some travelers may have clung to their buggies, but they were left behind in the dust—literally.

As a Social Media expert who helps entrepreneurs understand

and use Facebook to grow their businesses, I assure you this networking platform is here to stay. Facebook has skyrocketed far beyond its original vision (connecting college buddies) and now offers you an incredibly effective, affordable way to grow your business.

A Few Facts

Facebook is, well, humungous.

- At the time of this writing, Facebook has 500 million users, and is hands down the biggest social networking site on the planet.

- Its growth shows no signs of slowing, either, not with 1 million new users joining the throng every day.

- Most impressive is the rate at which Facebook users are active—half log in on any given day.

You may believe your target market isn't on Facebook; that only kids use it. And while Gen Y and X users do figure big, as of January 2010, the largest demographic on Facebook was over 35 years old. What's more, users ages 55 and older have exploded in the last two years.

Now, my inner marketing maven is jumping and shouting: This is too big of an opportunity you to ignore! And if you're not already marketing your business on Facebook, chances are good your competitors are. Why be left behind by plodding along at a snail's pace?

Don't wait—now is the time to shift your marketing mojo into high gear by understanding and leveraging the incredible power of Facebook.

7 Ways to Use Facebook for Business

Let's look at some specific ways you can use Facebook to grow a following. (I'm using "followers" and "fans" interchangeably—

both of which often turn into "customers."). These apply whether you're launching a new business, want to boost flagging sales or have a thriving company that you want to keep that way.

1. Create a Facebook Business (aka: Fan) Page

Just as we have social relationships with friends, thanks to tools like Facebook, we now have <u>social relationships with *companies*</u>. The way to open the door to your target market and nurture an ongoing relationship—both key aspects of marketing with social networks—is to create a Facebook business page.

This is a simple process that takes literally minutes. For specifics on how to set up a business page, I highly recommend *Facebook Marketing: An Hour a Day* by Chris Treadaway and Mari Smith. You can also see www.socialmediaexaminer.com, a quality site loaded with tips.

A Facebook business page can help you create a strong online presence that allows you to regularly touch base with your target market. Rather than simply getting a newsletter or postcard now and then, people receive get daily updates from you when you fill in the box on your page that says, "Write something…" (*What* to write we'll talk about in a sec.)

Clients often ask me if they need a separate business page if they already have a personal Facebook profile. Although there are varying opinions on this, I recommend <u>establishing your company separately</u>. This allows you to have a much more branded and focused page.

As you create your page, fill out your profile completely. Most important is the profile picture. This can be a logo or a picture of you, your product, or even your place of business. Having an image helps fans and potential fans know you're the real-deal—not a fake. We just don't trust something we can't see, so be sure to include a good image.

Power Tip: Launch your Facebook business page today. If you already have one, review your profile to be sure it's complete.

2. Develop Your Base of Fans or "Likes"

So, you have a Facebook business page. Now what? Time for the real work to begin!

Creating a page takes only minutes, but building a following takes deliberate, consistent action over weeks and months. That said, don't get discouraged—a little time every day *will* grow your fans.

An easy way to start is to invite your friends to fan your page. Then, think about all of your networks, email lists, blogs you read and any other place you are online. Give strong calls to action to invite people to "like" your page. If you know influential users—those with large networks—ask if they would be willing to help you spread the word. Growth comes quickly when you tap into key partners with substantial networks.

You can also spread word of your page by including your URL or a Facebook icon to every marketing vehicle you have: website, newsletter, brochures, postcards, even business cards. The more you shout out where you are on Facebook, the easier it is for interested folks to find you.

Promote your page on other networks such as Twitter and LinkedIn, too. Think of it as "radical visibility"—wherever your ideal client is, you want to be available. *Seen.* Don't be shy; shout it out!

Power Tip: Be diligent in growing your network to reap the most rewards.

3. Deliver Valuable Content

A main way to use your page is to deliver valuable content, tips, tools and information to your followers. This in turn will encourage them to interact with you—to comment on posts, share your page with friends, and ultimately to garner interest in your products or services.

Why is this so important? The average Facebook user has over 100 friends. When people comment on your page, a message on *their* page says you've commented. Thus, for every one comment, <u>an additional 100-plus people are exposed to your company name.</u> This is why posting valuable content is so important. It elicits more comments, gets you more visibility, and grows your fan base and influence.

Types of content to include on your Facebook page are varied and depend on you and your business. But a few ideas include:

- If you blog, you can post your latest articles on Facebook. This will not only offer your fans helpful information, it will guide them straight to your website. They may well subscribe to your blog, become a regular reader and turn into your next client or customer.

- Look for articles, tips, tools and other information your target market would benefit from, and tell them about it. You'll be offering something for nothing while building good customer-service karma.

- Is your store or business having a sale? Shout it out! Even better, give your Facebook fans a special discount, rewarding them for following your page.

- Pictures and videos of products, customers, staff, and events give followers an insider view of your company. Most importantly, you become human—more real—when share yourself and your company through images.

Power Tip: Make a point to share useful, helpful information. Your followers will respond!

4. Chat with Your Followers to Build Trust

Another form of content is conversation, which allows you to connect in a natural way with fans. This builds trust and interest in you as a person—and we all know the adage that we do business with those we like, know and trust.

I recently revamped the Social Media strategy of a company that sold food products to moms. They'd been posting heavy-duty marketing messages on Facebook to which they rarely if ever got a response.

My first step was to shift the tone from pushy marketing spiel to easy, casual conversation. I approached each update as if I were mom—a person whom the company's target market would relate. So, sprinkled between blog posts and helpful articles, I wrote updates like this: "Is it hard to get your kids to eat healthy stuff? Any tips to share?"

To followers, this company was no longer pushing products, but was interested in them, their opinions and thoughts. The floodgates of comments opened up and drove traffic to their website, where people then had an opportunity to purchase products.

Power Tip: Be conversational, not pushy, when using Facebook.

5. Listen to Your Customers to Gain Insight

Facebook offers a peek into what your customers think about you. In fact, it offers a built-in focus group right at your keyboard-fingertips!

As an example, Frost Doughnuts in Seattle uses Facebook to share their daily specials and to announce deals like "Frost Friday"—15 doughnuts for the price of 12. In return, fans load them up with feedback:

- "Thank you so much for the delicious chocolate French crullers! OMG, amazing!"
- "The pumpkin walnut fritter was so yummy!"
- "I'm so happy the fall flavors are back in!"

Customers are glad to offer ideas, too:

- "Do you take suggestions for new flavor combinations? My nine-year-old daughter has a winner—a bar topped with Nutella and sprinkled with hazelnuts. Her name is Anna and she's one of your biggest fans!" (Frost's reply: "We most definitely do! Tell Anna that sounds delicious—we will have to give it a try!")

- "I think you need to go national! We could use a Frost Doughnuts in the cultural district of Fort Worth. It would be a hit!" (Frost's reply: "You never know! It may just happen!")

Simply listening and responding to followers on Facebook creates a buzz about your business. In return, fans become more invested in your company, because they're already investing a precious commodity: their time.

Power Tip: Casual conversation offers loads of insight into how your customers thoughts.

6. Post Photos to Promote Sales

You can also create photo albums on your business page, which—used creatively—can drive sales straight to your website.

Seattle's Fusion Beads does this well. They invite customers to post photos of jewelry made with beads from their store. Not only is this good service to those looking for design ideas and inspiration, it showcases Fusion's products. Best of all, this is word-of-mouth marketing at its finest; customers are doing the selling for you.

Power Tip: Use images to help you sell and promote your stuff.

7. Customize with Facebook Application

Facebook has thousands of applications to customize your business page—and most are free and very easy to use.

- Do you want to build your email list? Add a "join my list" tab to your Facebook page complete with contact box.
- Create a customized "welcome" page for folks the first time they land on your Facebook page. The next time they visit, they'll go straight to your wall—the main gathering place where you interact with fans.
- You can easily add a poll to your page, gathering info from followers or simply increasing your engagement with them.
- Instead of creating expensive brochures, postcards or flyers, use Facebook's free events application. There's a handy RSVP function, so you know just who's coming, as well as an option for people to click "no" or "maybe."
- Add a YouTube video application to showcase some interesting aspect of your company. One of my favorite uses of this is a natural soap company that shows fans how they handcraft their soap, conveying the quality and luxury of their product.

Start Today!
Don't let another day go by without delving into how Facebook can help you market, grow, promote and gain visibility for your business. The possibilities for small business owners, entrepreneurs, and solopreneurs are simply unmatched, so open that door and get started!

About the Author: Lynn Baldwin-Rhoades founded Power Chicks International, an online community of entrepreneurs and professionals committed to real relationships and inspired success. She also founded Marketing Shebang and offers Social Media consulting to help businesses understand and leverage a thriving Facebook presence.

Contact Info:
Lynn Baldwin-Rhoades
www.powerchicksinternational.com
www.marketingshebang.com

CHAPTER TWELVE

YOUTUBE: 10 Tips for Mastering YouTube®

By David Steel

What is YouTube®?

YouTube® is an International web portal that takes video recording combined with social networking to a new level of all time. There is something genuine about seeing someone that has filmed themselves on a video. This sensationalism for people's lives began ages ago when the video camcorder enabled the world to share and record their lives with each other. Now YouTube has made it possible for people to post, comment, interact, and become a sensation through their video portal, whether videos are being posted to educate, inform, share, advertise, or for personal reasons.

YouTube's success can be credited to the fact that it has responded to the intense demand to have a visual medium where people of all backgrounds, locations, and cultures can share, communicate, watch, enjoy, and interact over their videos, channels, and captions. It has expanded what we thought we knew of videos, online marketing, and social networking.

YouTube is modern phenomenon made possible through the Internet's capabilities of reaching *everyone, everywhere*. It has expanded into an enormous social networking site for people to post videos on their own channels and enable others to subscribe, comment, and interact between users subscribe. Expressing oneself on a video brings out the true essence of an individual. You can see their body language, expressions, and see that they are indeed "real."

Anyone and everyone can use YouTube for their own purposes, and people are finding new means and ways that they can gain attention, traffic, and well…be the next big YouTube star and maybe even have their video go viral. However if you want to *master* YouTube, there are some tips in this chapter to assist you in making your videos and spreading the word more effectively for whatever your purpose may be.

With the access of easy to use pocket camcorders, and flip video cameras, anyone can make a video, and as a subscriber on YouTube anyone can post a video. However if you want to really understand how you can make YouTube work for you, you need to focus into more in-depth options for getting a fan base, enlarging your network, and getting the word out about what you have to offer with your videos, business, and websites.

Tip #1: It is All About the Content

If you know and understand anything about articles, advertising, websites, social networking, and other marketing options through the Internet, you have to know the vast importance of content. *It is all about the content!* SEO/SEM is crucial in order to have search engines pick up your keywords, tags, and videos on the vast space underneath thousands of other videos. If you have good content, and focus a bit on keywords, quality content, and tags, you will have the foundation to become more popular through cyberspace.

Approach your videos as you would anything else on the Internet, when it is along the lines of content. The sharper the content in your videos, the more interesting, and better search engine optimized and marketed they are, the better your endeavors to gain traffic, subscribers, comments, and increased visibility will be. This is a good start to mastering YouTube, but along with this priority there are many others that have to be integrated with content.

Tip #2: Spread the Word

When it comes to gaining popularity on YouTube, it starts with one individual who tells another, who then tells another to check it out. This is the **domino effect**. You can start this effect by contacting friends and acquaintances and telling them about your videos. Perhaps via phone or email, you can send them links to your channel or videos. You can also prompt and encourage them to comment, subscribe, and forward it on to their friends if they like what you are providing in your video.

By inviting your friends to view your videos, you are laying the foundation of a fan base, which is built upon the simple principle of **word of mouth**. The more people that come to visit you, the more comments are made in regards to the topic of interest of your videos, and the better it will be placed in onsite search rankings and by the search engines. You will gain popularity by this action alone; however there is still more to do.

Tip #3: Promoting and Advertising

When you get serious about your efforts on YouTube, you will find many options for advertising and promoting what you have to offer…whether it is to gain more traffic to your online business or website, or simply to be known as an expert in your field. YouTube does offer an ad campaign such as Google Adwords (it should not surprise you since Google owns YouTube). It allows you to advertise on other sites and through the Internet. That way, people can have links to your channels and videos whenever they fall upon a relevant category or topic. Remember, the goal is to have people subscribe to your channel so that you can market to them in the future without incurring additional advertising expense.

There are many ways that you can advertise on the 'net. But it is up to your personal budget, and how deep you want to get into advertising and promotion. You can also advertise and promote your videos to reach your niche on various targeted sites by contributing content or distributing content, and you may also want to find some affiliates once you get the right amount of traffic accumulated. This will be worth your while.

Two simple things you can do right away are post a link to your YouTube-channel on your website and include it in your email signature; every little bit helps!

Tip #4: Know your Purpose and Niche

If you understand what the main purpose in your videos are, you will better be fueled and equipped for targeting the audience that will be both captivated and interested in what you offer. For instance, if you sell products or services, you can supply informational videos or directional videos showing how you can assemble and/or use your products. Or you can demonstrate what your product does. Think of it as **your own personal infomercial.**

In another instance, perhaps there is a product that many retailers sell that you distribute. You may put together an instructional video and then proceed to enable other retailers and users to post the video and links to their site. You can also correspond and integrate your videos with other people that are in your same niche to gain more visibility and responses.

Tip #5: Other Social Networks

Among other tricks of gaining YouTube popularity is that of using and integrating other social networks into your game. LinkedIn, Digg-it, Facebook, MySpace, and Twitter can all be essential tools that you incorporate into your YouTube page and videos. You can have other accounts with social networks and post links and videos all over the Internet to spread the word further on what you have to offer.

You may also urge others to share your videos on their social networks when they like it. This enables you to capitalize and maximize your visibility throughout the Internet. You should make it a priority to integrate and interact with users and potential subscribers through other major social networks.

Tip #6: Profiles and Links

When you sign up for YouTube, a channel is automatically

created that has a profile. You can build this profile and make it more efficient for your purpose by including information such as your other social network links, website links, and links that may be of interest to others. You want a professional profile with as much information as possible that enables you to keep your privacy, but that intrigues others to get you maximum exposure.

Also you want to enable **links that are in working form**, so that those who are searching for a particular thing may be capable of finding it without hassle. This will assure that you keep ones interest, even if they choose not to watch your video- but want to contact and purchase the goods or services you provide.

Tip #7: How Often to Post Videos on YouTube

The ideal frequency for posting videos varies and will be dependent on the free time you have to dedicate to create, edit, and post those videos. It may also fluctuate according to the demand and supply mechanism; where you have a new product or feature and need to market that through the means of YouTube.

If you are not getting the viewership that you want on your channel, you may want to come up with a fresh perspective and post a video that will enlighten and engage your audience. Although, your other videos will still be on there and continue to draw traffic your way, it is best to consider new content as a boost to your entire purpose.

Tip #8: Snippets for Your Videos

Videos on YouTube <u>cannot be longer than ten-minutes</u>. So you want to include the best information you have on each video's specific topic. Basically, keeping it short and sweet is often the most appealing to others. You can achieve this by also investing in editing software which can grab the most important pieces of your different videos and use them as teasers to promote your videos (e.g. put the short snippets on your website with a link to the complete versions you posted on YouTube).

Snippets and clips are wise to stick within YouTube, because short videos often keep the audience interested and enable you to make a series of "compilation" videos later on that can be longer, and put on a DVD, or delivered as an online download, to sell on your website. You want your videos to look professional and when you *selectively* choose what is in your videos, it makes them much more attractive to others. This will definitely give you the edge on other video posters out there!

Tip #9: Automation

Automation is essential for promoting videos, especially for people who are uneducated on Social Media users. It is not considered cheating. *Robots for automating the YouTube process will enable you to more efficiently go on sites and gather people and followers, businesses, traffic, and visibility.* This gives you the ability to reach out to the individuals for them to watch, rate, comment, and interact with your videos. If the videos are very good, this also increases discovery of your videos and is a very effective technique and strategy…and is proven to be the best strategy.

What it entails is that you send them a message that suggests they take a look at your video. This is also legal and allowable by YouTube, as long as you adhere to their limits. Automation also allows you to target your audience and gain an enormous amount of promotion through a simplified means.

Tip #10: Be Real

Right now, the trend on YouTube is that of *reality*. You can make your video appealing to others by using basic editing tools, however (like reality TV), YouTube brings the essence of us *as humans* into the forefront. Seeing someone in their element or vulnerable per se is where the attraction turns into somewhat obsessive behavior for some. So do not be a fake on YouTube! Make it real, be real, and keep it real!

The more authentically that you present yourself, and your

video, the better off you will be. Traffic, comments, interaction, visibility, and popularity will come as you demonstrate your genuine uniqueness and define yourself among the rest. Oh, and do not forget to have fun!

With all of these helpful tips, there are some that you may already be aware of while others may be new to you. Try to do your best and incorporate all of them as a whole, and you will find that your YouTube venture will expand in ways you never would have imagined. Use social networking as a promotion means, integrate SEO into your formats, try automation, keep your videos real and freshly updated, and encourage others to visit your channel. You will find that the word will spread like wildfire if you use these strategies. You just may be surprised at how a few minor techniques can drive you to stardom within your niche…and *you* could be the next big YouTube sensation!

About the Author: Author, motivational speaker and sought-after sales coach, David Steel is one of the nation's leading experts on Sales Motivation, and actively uses Social Media to promote his brand and business. Widely recognized for his ability to energize sales teams and drive revenue results, David works with businesses and C-level executives on such issues as hiring the right sales people, compensation, goals and sales strategies. David also teaches highly effective sales management skills that fuel highly aggressive sales teams. And, he is the author of *The Care and Feeding of Highly Aggressive Sales People* (an Amazon bestseller).

Contact Info:
David Steel
DavidSteelLive.com

CHAPTER THIRTEEN

BLOGS: Build Your Brand & Business by Blogging

By Bill Gram-Reefer

A web log (aka blog) is one of the most affordable and effective ways you can take advantage of the Internet to help you build your brand and business. Blogs are easy to build and maintain, and you can do it for free. Business blogging is an excellent way to connect your business with customers, your community, your industry or trade, your vendors, plus partners and employees...*and did I mention that it's FREE?*

To get started, you can use a free hosting service like Blogger.com or Wordpress.com. Each of these hosting services offers free accounts where you can begin blogging with or without a domain name. Each offers basic layouts so you can get started quickly. Once you purchase a domain name—register your domain for two years or more, not one—both services allow you to promote your own domain name for your business like mywidgets.com instead of mywidgets.blogger.com.

Once you purchase your domain name, you can self-host your site and use free blogging platform like Wordpress, Typepad, or Joomla. You can also find an inexpensive and adequate Web Hosting Service for as little as $5-10 per month. I have used Wordpress since 2004 and recommend it. Typepad and Joomla are good choices, too, for a business blog.

Let's consider why you ought to use one of these software systems. First, 90% of websites never change and they are relegated to the function of an electronic brochure; the content is fixed. Boring. On the other hand, blogging software let's you easily update your company news once or twice a day or more. Blogging is dynamic in comparison to static websites. That's what makes them (hopefully) so compelling that people subscribe to your RSS feed or visit regularly to see what's new. Indeed, blogs are about "what's next!"

Secondly, most entrepreneurs and small businesses are probably illiterate when it comes to coding HTML and PHP. Perhaps you once paid some kid or a retired hobbyist to build a site for you. Where are they now when you want to add some major news about your company, or add a calendar of your public speaking engagements, or post a video clip of your own?

Instead of having a "roll your own" website—that may not be up to date or is so convoluted that the next geek you hire would not know where to start—a blogging platform like Wordpress installs **a standard and compliant blog template.** Wordpress is so well known and so widely used for self-hosted blogs that a whole industry has grown up around it with thousands of plugins that help add functionality including a calendar, related posts, recent comments, and YouTube clips.

Unlike with a "one-off" static website built in HTML, you'll always be able to find someone familiar with Wordpress to help you get started or help you take your site to the next level (polls, e-commerce, Google Adsense) when you're ready. And, there are more benefits that will be outlined below.

The Three Golden Rules of Blogging:

1. Post and Link: The content side of blogging is the most important aspect of your site. A blog enables you to serve existing customers as well as attract new ones. A blog is the perfect place to show off your expertise and why your brand is different and better. Writing articles around the key terms that make up your area of business or expertise will also help build visibility for your blog on the Internet as potential customers search for "widgets" or "widgets in MyTown."

By linking to additional sources or URLs, you offer a universe of more detailed information. These can be some WIKI pages, a trade group, some other expert, even a previous post on your own site that offers more information!

By building incoming links from other sites, you'll build the strength of your site. And there are safe, cheap, and easy ways to do this over time, e.g. invite other experts from your field to post on your site—their vanity alone will propel them to link to their article—and by taking part in conversations on other related sites.

2. Be Persistent and Consistent. Keep at it. Stay committed. Consistently optimize content around the key words for which you want your site to be known. Remember…subtle efforts get subtle results, and you don't want that!

Posting a new article once per week is probably the minimum to keep your audience coming back. If you already own a company with employees, encourage your employees to post articles on the site. Have a "Staff Favorites" feature so employees can show off their expertise, too. In fact, a great way to motivate existing employees and recruit new ones is to put a spotlight on your employees and write about them, their hard work, and expertise and related experience.

What's new? Announce new products, popular lines, or new services, and crow about industry certification achievements you receive. Plus, visitors love "how to" articles and you can also consider some variation of a "Top Ten" list customized to your audience. And, be sure to promote your special events.

Tell your audience about your participation in local community causes or a national non-profit campaign. Place their logos or trade certification emblems on your site and link to the sponsoring agencies with whom you partner for a good cause or that show recognition from your peers.

3. Be Relevant and Interesting. Write product reviews and industry news to let potential customers know your blog offers expert analysis, not just hype. Make your blog a "go to" site for your trade. Ask customers for their opinions—solicit them!—and encourage customers to write experiences about using your product or service. Invite industry colleagues to write about new trends in widgets or legislation affecting your business or trade group.

What can blogging do for me?

By posting keyword optimized articles, news, events, and commentary on your blog and attracting incoming links, your site will begin to be more useful to your audience. Just as importantly, your site will earn more visibility on the Internet! Your blog and articles will begin to appear on the top pages of Bing, Google, and Yahoo searches for the key terms for which you've optimized your site. Gaining traction in Google and other search results will produce more eyeballs looking at your site over time.

How you convert those eyeballs into a new relationship, action, or sale is another matter. The basics include some easy first steps. Start with offering a free download of some premium content, in the form of an e-book, PowerPoint, or PDF file, in exchange for (at least) a visitor's e-mail address. Wordpress and other blogging platforms even have plugins that offers a CALL BACK button that enables a visitor to talk to you on the phone almost immediately.

Installing an idiot-proof and easy to use e-commerce plugin helps seal the deal if you are selling merchandise online. Turn on comments! Ask people to subscribe by e-mail or to your RSS feed that sends out each new posting. Make it easy for visitors to join conversations. Turn on "Comments" or offer a Chat system like Envolve.com that offers an easy Facebook-like chat interface.

Blogs can payoff for sellers of widgets that can ship all over the world as well as for local retail widget sellers. In fact, a study by Jupiter (2007) concludes that the Internet will impact sales **in stores** by $1 trillion in 2011, alone. Additionally, research (Centro 2005) shows 92% of customers shop online and 95% buy in the local brick and mortar retail store 92-95. Whether you sell widgets to customers globally, or just in MyTown, your blog is the best, easiest, and most affordable way to be in the right place at the right time.

Authors and service providers, especially real estate pros, can also use their blog to promote their avocation, business, and service. In fact, Real Estate Business Services that invite viewers to a virtual 360° walk-thru of a property already make up 22.5% of "Local-to-Local" online advertising (source: Borrell 2006)!

Also, experts in fields like environmental science, therapies and play time activities for kids with ADD or PSD, International Relations, life-coaching, and even hobbyists like Pittsburgh Steelers buffs, all use blogs to write about news, stats, and trends, to show off their expertise. You can too!

Making your blog visible is easy, too; especially with Wordpress. This is called Search Engine Optimization (SEO). In short SEO helps Google find and index your blog's pages so your site or article, or embedded video clip, show up not only near or at the top of the first page, but ubiquitously. This visibility helps you attract visitors that are actively searching for terms and phrases around your web site's focus. The more pages around these key terms are indexed by search engines, the more opportunity you have to be seen.

There are two important aspects to SEO. An advanced blogging platform like Wordpress will help you with the onsite mechanics side of the equation. For instance, there is a very popular and free plug-in for Wordpress, the All-In-One-SEO (AIO), that gathers most of the key elements into one dashboard.

It's one thing to have someone develop a one-off site by hand that may have title, description, and keyword content about your site on your home page. But AIO for Wordpress sites and blogs automates that process of building "meta data" not only for your home page, but for **every** post and page on your site! This is why many people are now choosing Wordpress for their website platform; not just their blogs!

So when you post a review of a new book on "*Understanding Your Widget,*" AIO automatically inserts your custom titles, descriptions, and other meta tags into the HTML for the post page. Depending on the density of the terms, your blog post can get the attention of Google quickly and possibly rank at the top of a search engine report page (SERP).

The other side of SEO is your content. Optimizing your content for search engines is critical. Focus on the title, description and first paragraph of every post. Make sure the title lets people and Google know what the post is about. A title like, "Oh No, Not Again!" means NOTHING to your reader or Google. Alternatively, a title like, "New Widgets in My Town's Stores for Christmas Shopping," will get that page indexed properly so a search for "Widgets+ MyTown" will not only tell your readers exactly what the post is about, but Google will love it, especially for local search!

Write good titles (headlines and sub-heads) and focused copy, especially in your first paragraph. Lead with the key terms. Put the rambling, but mildly amusing story about Uncle Charlie during Christmas 1967, toward the bottom as an aside; don't put it at the top.

Another critical element for your articles is adding graphic images. Pictures tell a thousand words for sure, but they also help attract attention on a web site or blog, especially close-ups! On the behind-the-scenes SEO side, make sure to rename an image from whatever gibberish the camera creates for a file name like IMG_084587.jpg. Instead name the image "MyTown_Widgets.jpg," and put the key terms you enter in AIO for the post into the ALT tag section of the HTML that embeds the image into your post. Since images usually appear at the top of posts, now Google will see even more key terms near the top. Bottom-line? The file names you give your pics are searchable online, so why not take the time to use keywords when naming them?

Finally, Wordpress also makes it easy to integrate your blog with your existing or new social networks like Twitter, Facebook fan pages, and LinkedIn. Plug-ins are available that will show tweets or comments from your followers on Twitter or Facebook on your own site using a widget in the sidebar of you blog. Conversely you can send your blog posts or embed your current home page or "RSS feed" on Facebook, Twitter, or LinkedIn so friends can read your articles while visiting Facebook or LinkedIn.

Finding ways that help "complete the circle" between your blog, social networks, and Google will help you build your visibility, visitors, and reputation...and that will build your brand and business!

About the Author: Bill Gram-Reefer is an expert on the Search Engine Optimization of Press Releases to help clients make their news highly visible on the Internet and Social Media networks. WORLDVIEW PR, founded by Bill in 2001, serves a wide variety of clients including technology, consumer electronics, the wine and beverage industries, non-profits, and public affairs, to name just a few. In addition to expert SEO, Gram-Reefer is a skilled public relations professional that delivers media-relations results for customers. Bill also publishes Halfway To Concord, the leading independent political blog in Contra Costa County, and the East Bay of Northern California.

Contact Info:
Bill Gram-Reefer
WORLDVIEW PR, Traditional PR and SEO
reefer@worldviewpr.com
http://worldviewpr.com; http://halfwaytoconcord.com
925-323-3169
LinkedIn: Bill Gram-Reefer; Twitter: halfway2concord

CHAPTER FOURTEEN

Your A-Z Guide of Social Media and Business Communication

By Susan Young

The way you communicate in your business relationships is directly tied to your revenues, reputation and success. Of course Social Media and technology are forcing us to set new rules, boundaries and etiquette. Back to grade school we go!

Here are the ABC's of Outstanding Social Media and Business Communication:

A is for authenticity. In the case of Social Media and online networking, the old adage "Fake it 'til you make it" doesn't work. Genuine is in; fake is out. Be yourself; be real.

B is for brand. Every message, tweet, blog and communication should reflect some hint of your brand and who you are.

C is for control yourself. Be careful not to slam or insult anyone online as it can come back to bite you in ways you never imagined.

D is for dialogue. Get involved in the conversations, groups and chats with meaningful contributions that reveal both your expertise and personality. Communication is a two-way street.

E is for easy does it. Before you jump into conversations or new arenas, take a look around. Follow chats, Tweets and groups. Find the opinion leaders, and movers and shakers. Then slowly get involved.

F is for forge relationships. Pay attention to your loyal followers, ideal client targets and competition. Thank those who retweet or share your information with others and connect with them offline. Follow what others are doing and comment on their blogs and sites. Interactive is a beautiful thing.

G is for get in front. This is about being proactive and making things happen. It's not about being aggressive, obnoxious or "in your face." It's subtle marketing, branding and sharing value—online.

H is for headlines. Catchy news-style headlines of 5-8 words (including keywords) that address people's needs/challenges will attract readers and followers, and help your SEO efforts.

I is for identify. Identify your niche. Identify your area of expertise and passion. Identify industry leaders. Identify trends in your field. Identify your ideal clients. Determine where they "hang out" online and go there. Watch them. We are in an amazing age where we can get access to CEO's, prominent business leaders and superstars that we never could have mingled with before. And don't forget, identify your competition and watch them too.

J is for just get going. Don't whine that blogging takes too much time, or you'll have to learn new technology. Look at Social Media and online networking as a breakthrough opportunity that the world has never experienced. Imagine the stories you'll tell your grandchildren! If you want to bellyache instead of learn, get back in bed and pull the covers over your head. Everyone else is going places. It would be nice if you came along.

K is for knowledge. Know your followers, why they connect with you and what you provide to them. Then give them more of what they want. If you don't know, start asking them.

L is for limit your personal life when doing business. It's great to share your personal insights or "Lessons Learned" but too much information about your private life when you are online to build your business reputation can backfire and destroy your credibility.

M is for mistakes. You're bound to send out a message with a wrong link or misspelled word. Fix it if necessary; send out a correction or apology, if appropriate, and move on. It happens to everyone. The nice thing about Social Media, especially Twitter, is that it's a very forgiving community :)

N is for notice the little things. Someone may tweet or post a message about their birthday, the flu, or their upcoming presentation. A few quick words wishing them good luck, or asking about the topic of their workshop helps build relationships. People appreciate being recognized.

O is for own it. Be passionate about what you do. Your enthusiasm will leak into all of your spoken and written words. Friends, Followers, and Connections will pick up on this immediately. If you don't own it and love it, it's time to reassess what you're doing, and why.

P is for professional. Use your profiles, posts, and messages in professional ways. Present yourself online to prospects, clients and the world as a top-notch pro that walks the walk and talks the talk. This should be evident in all of your Social Media communication. It must be congruent with your traditional marketing materials, website, articles, and press releases.

Q is for quit trying to sell. If you post a link that offers tips, make sure it leads to a page with the information you promised, not a sales pitch to buy your book or register for a webinar to get the tips.

R is for rapport. Connect with people through your blog, posts, links, articles, e-zines and videos. Give them an opportunity to get acquainted with you. Developing friendships online is similar to real-life friendships. You'll connect with some people immediately and others take more time. There are a few you will never click with. That's ok. Go for quality not quantity.

S is for sharing. Share your expertise, insights, wisdom and assistance. That's what the community of Social Media is all about. Be willing to donate the seeds of your intellectual capital, knowing you are building a brand and reputation that will eventually take root. In other words, share your smarts but don't expect an instant ROI (return on investment).

T is for thank you. Express your gratitude and thanks to people who provide helpful information, share your messages, posts and tweets with their circles, and comment on your blog or LinkedIn questions.

U is for use everything that's available. Don't get nervous. You don't have to use all of the applications, gadgets, downloads and software at the same time and right now. Commit to learning a new technology or program and build from that. Use these tools to your advantage as you grow your business and online presence.

V is for visuals. Social Media is interactive. There are different ways that people learn and communicate. Use a broad approach to include various styles and age groups. You can post an E-brochure on your site that allows people to see and hear your style and approach. You can record a video blog or podcast. Get creative!

W is for write with clarity. Whether you are writing a white paper, a short blog post, or a question on Linked In, use language that is clear, concise and compelling.

X is for the "X-Ray Approach." In order to effectively communicate and relate to people, you'll need to get inside their heads and emotions. Read their materials, listen to their seminars, and ask good questions. You'll soon be able to diagnose their pain (challenge) and determine if your products and services will be the cure.

Y is for yell if you need any help. People love to help. Periodically toss out your questions or challenges to the crowd and allow them to connect with you. Tap into their experiences, ideas and resources to help with your learning curve.

Z is for zany. Sure I talk about being professional and sharing your personality, but you can let your hair down in a zany and fun way. For example, on Christmas, my blog post was titled "Santa's Communication Pitfalls." On Halloween, I blogged about "Scary

Customer Service." Maybe it's not totally zany, but you get the picture. It's ok to have fun!

Communicating online requires us to write the line, walk the line, read between the lines and often tow the line. Are you up for it? It can be as easy as A-B-C!

About the Author: Susan Young works with professionals who want to supercharge their communication skills, self-confidence, and success. She is the President of Get in Front Communications, Inc., a public relations and communications training company. Susan also provides presentations and coaching on sales, reading body language, emotional intelligence, and Social Media.

Contact Info:
Susan Young
www.getinfrontblogging.com
www.getinfrontcommunications.com
Twitter @sueyoungmedia

Promote U & Increase Your Income Thru
Other Cool Tools

"No matter what your product is, you are ultimately in the education business. Your customers need to be constantly educated about the many advantages of doing business with you, trained to use your products more effectively, and taught how to make never-ending improvement in their lives."

~ Robert G Allen
Business, Finance & Motivational Author and Co-author of the best selling books: *The One Minute Millionaire* and *Cracking the Millionaire Code*

INTRODUCTION TO PART FOUR

Promote U & Increase Your Income Thru Other Cool Tools

Is your head ready to explode after reading that info-packed section on Social Media? I hope you took notes or keep this book for reference because it will save you tons of time as you get started using Social Media in your marketing mix. Why learn through endless hours of trial and error when you just had EIGHT experts share tips that can help ramp your efforts faster?

On the partition page for Part Three I shared a quote from Matt Dickman that began with, "*Social Media isn't the end-all-be-all…*" I'm mentioning this again because it's true. Social Media is simply another marketing and branding tool to add to your overall mix.

There are many other tools outside of traditional Social Media strategies that will not only get you mass exposure, attract clients, foster media inquiries, and land income opportunities (such as speaking engagements), but that can also create multiple streams of income for you. And in Part Four we're going to explore those!

Also, as with Part Three, there are several top experts who will be your "teachers" in the following pages. They are: Jim Palmer, The Newsletter Guru; Lee B. Salz, Founder and CEO of Business Expert Webinars; Pamela Cox, President of Pamela Cox Email Marketing; Kathleen Gage, Founder of The Street Smarts Marketing System; Vicki Flaugher, Online Marketing Strategist; Diane Marie Pinkard, Sales Expert & Trainer; and Sponsorship Expert, Linda Hollander, the Wealthy Bag Lady.

We have a lot to cover in Part Four, so turn the page and let's get going!

CHAPTER FIFTEEN

How to Create an Everlasting Bond with Your Customers So They Spend More, Stay Longer, and Refer More!

By Jim Palmer

I have 30 years of experience in marketing and growing businesses with newsletters, both for my previous employers and now for my hundreds of clients and customers in seven different countries. Based on that experience, I am 100-percent confident that if you follow my advice and suggestions, and are not what I refer to as a newsletter pansy, you will see more profits and customers for life in your business—*no matter what business you are in!*

My belief in friendly customer newsletters as an amazing—almost magical—marketing tool is so strong that in 2001, when I decided to go into business for myself, I knew that newsletters would be my main offering. And what a ride it has been!

My belief in friendly customer newsletters is so strong that I believe anyone who doesn't mail a monthly newsletter to their customers is simply being a newsletter pansy. There is simply too much empirical evidence and data that prove my case.

It's a fact that customer newsletters help businesses succeed. And the best and most effective way to grow your business, boost your profits, and get more customers for life is to mail monthly. There really is no better way to develop a relationship with people than sending out a properly written monthly newsletter.

Dollar for dollar, newsletters are the most effective marketing tool available. Plus, customers who read your newsletter are usually in a good position to do business with you again and recommend your product or service to others. And that's where your new business comes from! Let me share with you more of what I call the magic of newsletter marketing.

Newsletters are not perceived in the same manner as are post-cards, fliers, or other forms of direct mail marketing. When people receive these or anything else that has a sales and marketing feel to it, their guard goes up and they think, "Uh-oh. What are they trying to sell me?"

Newsletters work well because they tend to be read as informational, making them more welcome when they are received. As such, they have **higher readership than other forms of advertising.** People also tend to be more receptive to what you have to say in your newsletter, because newsletters aren't meant to be sales tools. Rather, they are designed to be an information resource.

Marketing genius Dan Kennedy put it this way: "People are conditioned to be less resistant to reading information such as articles than they are advertising." Because people are conditioned to be less resistant to reading information, which is exactly what a newsletter should be, most people read a newsletter with their guard down. This is a HUGE marketing advantage. When your customers' guard is down, they are open and receptive to what you have to say!

That is the magic of why newsletters are such an effective marketing tool. People don't realize that they're actually reading something that's going to cause them to buy…*if* the newsletter is done correctly. That's the big caveat here. To learn more about creating a great newsletter that gets results, I invite you to get a copy of my book, *The Magic of Newsletter Marketing—The Secret to More Profits and Customers for Life!* This book will help you; it's the wand that will open doors and bring you customers.

Now I want to share with you seven of the many proven ways that newsletters will help your business grow.

Secret 1: Newsletters Help Keep Existing Customers

Your current customers hold the best prospects for future growth. Plus, the longer they are customers, the more likely they are to spend with you.

A monthly company newsletter helps you stay top-of-mind with your current customers. When your newsletter arrives, your customers start to think about you. Issue after issue, your newsletter reinforces your relationship with your customers and gives you a way to tell them about products and services they may not know about.

Secret 2: Newsletters Help Get New Customers

You want your newsletter to help you get new customers. Informative articles give your newsletter what marketing pros call "pass-along value." Your newsletter makes it easy to pass on the information. Because people read newsletters as a publication and not as a marketing piece, a newsletter is a great way to tell potential customers about your business.

Secret 3: Newsletters Help Build Credibility

When people read your brochure, they treat it as a piece of marketing literature. But when they read your newsletter, they treat it as a publication. Your newsletter also gives you the opportunity to tell people success stories about what you do and how well your products work. You can illustrate the benefits of your product or service with statistics and customer testimonials.

Credibility is a huge benefit of a monthly printed newsletter. Listen to what Nick Nanton, the celebrity lawyer and best-selling author of *Celebrity Branding You*, says: "I didn't believe it either. But adding a hard-copy newsletter to my business was the best thing I ever did. It increased my credibility, visibility, and profitability virtually overnight. If you don't have a newsletter, you're making a huge mistake by missing the opportunity to develop a deeper relationship with your prospects and clients for maximum profitability."

Secret 4: Newsletters Help You Stand Out from Your Competition

Since you decide the direction and content of each newsletter, you can differentiate yourself from others—especially the larger businesses that typically do not produce customer newsletters.

Secret 5: Newsletters Enhance Your Reputation

Your customers may not be ready for or need your product or service today, but when they are, they want an experienced professional. People want to do business with someone they know, like, and trust, so when they are ready for what you offer, they'll turn to you.

Secret 6: Newsletters Help You Build Your Brand

Branding is the art of making people aware of who you are, what you do, and how you're different from and better than the competition. You want to have a little bell go off in people's heads when they hear your name. You want them to say, "Oh, yes, they're the people who…"

When your newsletter is delivered at the same time each month, it builds up a level of importance. It helps build your brand, which helps your business grow.

Secret 7: Newsletters Have a Longer Shelf Life than Other Types of Marketing

Newsletters are portable; they go everywhere. Newsletters that are informative, fun, and easy to read are not thrown away. People pass along newsletters to friends, business associates, or even neighbors. This is a *huge* benefit of producing a newsletter.

The question many people ask is, "Why publish a customer newsletter every month?" If nothing I have written so far makes any sense, let me give you a little straight talk. The reason that you mail your customers a print newsletter every month is because it works! **It works BIG TIME!**

Publishing a customer newsletter every month is simply *the right thing to do* for your business. Just like changing the oil in your car every three thousand miles. When you change the oil in your car, you don't see or feel any immediate gratification—you do it because it will make your car last longer and serve you better. It's the right thing to do.

It's like that with a newsletter. You publish a newsletter every month because it's the right thing to do for your business. Much of the time you won't see any immediate gratification. Customers may not mention that they like your newsletter, and you may not hear your cash register ring more often immediately after mailing it. But it is the right thing to do for your business, and doing so month in and month out like clockwork is the surest way I know to boost your profits and get more customers for life.

To ignore this reality and do anything less is being a newsletter pansy and potentially harming your business by not maximizing the profit potential of each and every customer.

Here's what I know about newsletter marketing after three decades of experience: The companies that publish a monthly newsletter regularly, month in and month out like clockwork, have stronger, longer-lasting, and more profitable relationships with their customers and clients. And, as history has shown, they have <u>more repeat and referral</u> business.

You might be wondering why I suggest that you focus so much of your time and effort on current customers rather than on new customers. I'm glad you asked. Let me introduce you to Jim Palmer's 80/20 Rule of Marketing ...

No doubt you've heard of the 80/20 rule that says 80-percent of your profits come from 20-percent of your customers. I believe that, and so should you—it's the truth. I contend that smart entrepreneurs and business owners should focus more of their marketing time and resources on nurturing, developing, and growing the customer relationships that they already have instead of constantly trying to acquire new customers. It costs more and takes longer to acquire and sell to a new customer than it does to sell more to current customers.

Most businesses spend the majority of their marketing time and resources trying to acquire *new* customers. That makes no sense. It is so much easier and quicker to sell more to your current customers.

So the right thing to do is to spend a majority of your marketing dollars continuing to grow and maximize the profitability of *existing* customer relationships. You already have an established relationship with your current customers, and they have already purchased from you. This means that they find value in what you're selling and they trust you. This is a huge hurdle that we all have to overcome when we are prospecting for new customers—a hurdle that you've already overcome with your current customers.

So once you've invested the time, effort, and expense of acquiring these customers, the right thing to do for your business is to *maximize the profitability* of your customer relationships.

Again, a monthly customer newsletter helps you stay top-of-mind with your current customers! Your newsletter arrives, and instantly your customers are thinking about you. After receiving your newsletter on a consistent basis, your customers actually begin to look forward to receiving it—it's a welcome friend—and they are curious to see what tips and stories you are sharing with them in the newest issue.

Issue after issue, your newsletter reinforces your relationship with your customers. It makes your connection with them stronger. It also gives you a way to tell current customers about products and services you provide that they may not know about.

So there you have it—I simply can't say it any more clearly!

Publishing a monthly customer newsletter is smart. Not doing so, no matter what business you're in, is simply being (again) a newsletter pansy.

You may be asking, "If newsletters are such a powerful marketing tool, then why doesn't every business use one?" I'm glad you asked; that's an easy question to answer. The fact is, newsletters can be difficult and time consuming to produce. That's why most companies that say that they have a "monthly" newsletter send it out…*only three to four times per year!*

When asked why they don't do it more consistently, the top two reasons given are:

1.) They take too long to produce.
2.) I'm always struggling to find content (what to put in the newsletter).

Perhaps this may be why you are not yet sending your customers a monthly newsletter, following the successful and proven path to growth and higher profits that so many before you have. Am I right? And let's face it—as entrepreneurs, we're already wearing many other hats, and when push comes to shove, the newsletter always seems to get pushed to the back burner or, worse yet, completely off the stove!

If this has been your experience and what has been holding you back, I invite you to check out my wildly popular "Done-By-Us-For-You" newsletter program called No Hassle Newsletters. Every month I provide subscribers with ready-to-go No Hassle Newsletter templates and a huge 24-page assortment of my 'Famous Customer-loving™ content. Learn more at www.NoHassleNewsletters.com.

Author the Author: Jim Palmer is an entrepreneur, author, speaker, and coach to other entrepreneurs. Jim is internationally known as The Newsletter Guru, the go-to expert for smart, effective strategies that maximize the profitability of customer relationships. He is also the acclaimed author of *The Magic of Newsletter Marketing—The Secret to More Profits and Customers for Life* and his latest book *Stick Like Glue - How to Create an Everlasting Bond with Your Customers So They Spend More, Stay Longer, and Refer More!* Get a 'boatload' of smart marketing and business building advice from Jim at NewsletterGuru.TV. And for a free newsletter template, 20-page special report, and more information on Jim and his companies, visit: TheNewsletterGuru.com.

Contact Info:
Jim Palmer
www.NewsletterGuru.TV
www.TheNewsletterGuru.com
www.Facebook.com/TheNewsletterGuru

CHAPTER SIXTEEN

Leveraging Webinars to Grow Your Business

By Lee B. Salz

You've been intrigued by webinars (*seminars delivered online with both audio and visual components and attended via your computer*), maybe even participated in some, but haven't yet taken the plunge to start delivering them yourself.

Right now, the webinar industry is booming, and it will continue to! From the attendees' perspective, it is very easy for them to participate as there is no travel involved. Many companies have reduced or eliminated their training budgets which make webinars a cost-effective alternative for employee skill development.

From the consultants', speakers' and trainers' perspective, it is an effective way to reach audiences, build brand, and generate income without much cost. Webinars allow you to reach people all around the globe, demonstrate your expertise, and create a new prospect pool.

Certainly, the economy has played a major role in exposing the benefits of webinars for both speakers and attendees which is why you should analyze the webinar opportunity for your business. As you plan your webinar strategy, one of the first decisions to make is whether you will deliver them *free* or *as **attendee-funded webinars (AFWs)**.*

Making the Decision: Free vs. For-Fee Webinars

Many people think of webinars as free events … and many virtual events are free to participants. However, webinars are also delivered on an attendee-funded basis (attendees paying to participate in the virtual event). Thus, one of the first decisions to make is whether you want to pursue the *free* or *for-fee* (aka: *AFW*) strategy.

Free webinars are often used to build mailing lists, establish brand awareness, or position products/services. While the expression is "free webinar," this only means that there is no charge to the attendees. As the speaker, you will have costs which include, but are not limited to: copywriting services, webinar technology, advertising, and your time to promote the event. One of the important considerations is the return on investment relative to your time and cash outlay for this initiative when "market exposure" is your sole compensation.

For-fee (attendee-funded) webinars are growing in popularity. Consultants, speakers and trainers are recognizing that they can effectively use webinar technology to share their expertise. Yet, "market exposure" is not the compensation they desire. They are pursuing this strategy to develop a new revenue stream for their business. These speakers get paid for every registrant in their webinars.

While you will usually have more attendees in a free webinar than you will in an attendee-funded one, the for-fee strategy oftentimes is a more beneficial approach as it serves as a lead funnel. The free webinar attendees have paid nothing to participate in the session. However, those in an AFW have made an investment to access the event. Thus, AFW attendees have demonstrated that they are motivated to tackle a particular issue and are willing to spend some dollars to solve it … making them a stronger lead source for your other services.

As you evaluate your free versus for-fee strategy, keep in mind that not all webinars are saleable. For example, if you have written a book and plan to deliver a webinar based on the book (and even use the book title as the webinar title), this should be offered as a *free* webinar. No one is going to pay to hear an infomercial about your book. Prospective attendees know that there is only so much you can cover in a 60-minute event and will not pay for an information buffet.

If you plan to pursue the AFW (charge a fee to attend) strategy, a book is a powerful credibility piece to *drive registrations*. Select a chapter, then take the audience on a journey beyond the pages and provide a training webinar that teaches actionable skills related to the chapter's topic. **People readily pay for training, but not for an infomercial.**

Depending on your free versus for-fee webinar strategy, your marketing timeline will vary. With free webinars, people register if they are intrigued by the event when they first hear about it. Yet, only 25% of the registrants attend free webinars. With AFWs, people do not register early. Most paid registrations occur within 48 hours of the virtual event. The challenge with AFWs is motivating people to buy a virtual seat and over 95% of registrants will attend the event. After all, they've paid to participate in the virtual course.

Some consultants, speakers and trainers try to offer both free and for-fee webinars, but this strategy often backfires on them. This month, you promote a free webinar to your clients. Next month, you offer an AFW. The following month, it's free again. While you may clearly understand why you offer some webinars for free and others for-fee, your clients will not follow this logic. They started off loving you, but they may come to resent you because your marketing seems deceptive. Pick one strategy and stick to it!

The Three Registrant Types ... And How to Engage Them

As you develop your webinar strategy, you will encounter three prospective registrant types: *Fans, Acquaintances, and Strangers*, and each requires a unique approach to capture their attention.

Fans are those who know you so well that you have their contact information. They are on your mailing list. They are your clients. While webinars may be new to you, don't expect them to be interested in the same content that made them *Fans* in the first place. This is particularly important if you are pursuing an AFW strategy. Many get excited about their new webinar program, offer the same content that they delivered in-person and are disappointed in the registration results. Fans don't want the same content again.

They want new, but related, content from you. If you've delivered Level 101, use your webinar program to deliver Level 201. If you've delivered a broad-brush keynote, use your campaign to hone-in on a few pertinent aspects from the speech.

At the other end of the registrant spectrum is the **Strangers** group. This prospective registrant type is introduced to you for the first time when they hear of your webinar. Whether you are asking for the investment of time (free) or dollars (for-fee), the *Strangers* ask themselves one fundamental question when determining whether or not to learn from you.

What makes you an expert on this subject matter…a thought leader? If you do not have <u>demonstrable expertise</u> on the topic you plan to deliver, you may want to reconsider your webinar course selection strategy. Demonstrable expertise comes in multiple forms including: well-experienced consultant, book authorship, academic credentials, etc. The webinar description you use to promote the virtual event should clearly position your expertise on the subject or it will be challenging to engage the *Strangers*.

A helpful tool is the use of testimonials of others who have gained knowledge from you on this subject and the results they have achieved as a result of your teachings. This experience does not have to be in a webinar environment, but should be content-related.

The **Acquaintance** group is often forgotten as a registrant source. These are people who have had some familiarity with you, but the challenge you face is not having their contact information. *Acquaintances* are your former audiences from your keynote speeches and association/professional group colleagues. Since they have already experienced you, they are an important group to re-engage as they will be more responsive than the *Strangers*. To leverage this webinar prospect type, if you are offering a free webinar, ask the organization coordinator to inform their members of your upcoming event as an act of goodwill. If you are offering an AFW, offer a commission to the organization for the registrations they generate.

Selecting the Right Webinar Provider for Your Campaign

With your webinar strategy selected, the next step is to select the right webinar provider for your campaign. While you may have only been exposed to a few webinar providers, there are actually hundreds of firms that offer webinar technology and services. Before evaluating webinar providers, determine your needs for your webinar campaign. Keep in mind that the attendees' webinar experience is a direct reflection on you and your business so make sure you perform a thorough due diligence when making your webinar provider choice.

• *Registration Management:* Whether you choose to pursue the free or AFW strategy, you need a way to register attendees for your webinars. Most webinar providers offer a registration page and some allow you to edit/customize the content. If you are pursuing an AFW strategy, you also need a way to process payment. While you may have your own electronic shopping cart to process payment or use a service (i.e., PayPal), it is most efficient if the webinar provider has integrated technology between registration and payment processing.

• *Event Management:* During your webinar provider evaluation, you will find webinar companies who "rent empty virtual rooms" and others who offer staffed events. Depending upon your needs, you may want to select a webinar provider that offers: a host for your webinars, personal training on the use of their technology, dissemination of participant handouts, and administration of surveys. If you don't need the additional bells and whistles, don't make it part of your scope as you could be increasing your costs.

• *Audio Services:* Another consideration is how the audio portion of your webinar is provided to participants. You may be tempted to require an 800 number, but that increases your cost and offers little value to the participants. Years ago, long distance charges were such that it was seen as a benefit if the event host provided an 800 number. Today, most people have unlimited long distance access at home and few are concerned about the cost in the workplace.

If you plan to offer AFWs, one of your decision points is the use of unique PIN (Personal Identification Number) codes. With free webinars, you don't mind if many people join your webinar using the same code. The goal is to have as many attendees as possible join the event. With AFWs, the webinar provider should have technology in place to control access to the virtual event so that only paid attendees join.

The other area to consider with respect to audio services is the way the participants hear the event. To be seen as cutting-edge, many want to offer sound only through computer speakers which brings about a number of potential issues. First, not everyone has computer speakers. Second, if there is any Internet latency among the speaker, attendee or webinar provider, the experience could be miserable for the attendee. Third, if you plan to verbally engage the attendees, most webinar technologies do not have the ability for the attendees to talk through their computer microphones.

• *Recording Capability:* Are you planning to record the event? If so, you need a provider that offers this functionality. For free webinars, you can send the recording to those who missed the event. With *AFWs*, the recording provides you with a product you can sell … another revenue stream.

• *Presenter Tools:* As the presenter of the webinar, you may desire tools beyond your PowerPoint presentation. Many webinar providers offer virtual white boards so you can point to content, draw, and highlight during the presentation. Others offer the additional functionality of sharing a desktop, showing a website, or demonstrating an application. Another tool to look for is polling—technology that allows you to ask a multiple choice question of your virtual audience and share the results. Not all webinar firms offer this technology. Before analyzing this aspect, be sure to determine the scope of your webinar so you know what tools you need.

• *Technology Requirements:* The visual portion of the webinar is delivered through the Internet. Some webinar technologies require speakers and participants to download software to join the webinar while others do not. This can be an issue as many workplaces do not permit employees to install software on their office computers. This means, if you are using technology that requires a software installation, a percentage of your attendees will not be able to access the event. If access is a significant concern of yours, select a webinar provider that does not require a software installation to participate in your virtual events.

Last, but not least, not all webinar technologies work *with both PCs and Macs.* While you may *not* be concerned about this because you use a PC, keep in mind that your attendees may be using an Apple brand computer. If you feel you have a significant number of attendees that use a Mac, select a webinar provider that can demonstrate a great experience for Mac users *and* PC users.

Regardless of whether you choose the free or for-fee path, webinars are a wonderful addition to a consultant, speaker, and trainer's portfolio. Not only will webinar help build your brand and generate leads, but they could also be the revenue source for which you've been searching.

About the Author: Lee B. Salz is the recognized authority on attendee-funded webinars. He is the Founder and CEO of Business Expert Webinars and the author of the widely-acclaimed book *Stop Speaking for Free! The Ultimate Guide to Making Money with Webinars.* He has helped hundreds of speakers, authors, trainers, and consultants stop giving away their content away for free and make money delivering attendee-funded webinars. The presentation is virtual but the dollars are real.

Contact Info:
Lee B. Salz
BusinessExpertWebinars.com
lsalz@BusinessExpertWebinars.com
763.416.4321

CHAPTER SEVENTEEN

The Five D's of An Effective Email Marketing Campaign

By Pamela Cox

Email marketing is a cost effective way to communicate directly with your customers and prospects and can be a powerful marketing tool when done right. Effective email marketing is more than just putting text in a template and hitting send. It is sending **the right message to the right audience at the right time.**

It sounds simple enough, but being the foodie that I am, I'll compare it to a fabulous meal. The end result is a perfect melding of flavors and a pleasing presentation, however the process to achieve that result requires careful planning, preparation, and testing. Just like a fabulous meal, an email marketing campaign has components that must come together as a whole for it to be successful.

The five essential components to an effective email marketing campaign are direction (plan), detail (content), design, database, and delivery. In this chapter, I'll discuss each of these components and their importance.

1. Direction (Plan):

An effective email marketing campaign begins with a plan that clearly states the purpose of the campaign and sets measurable goals. Before sending out your first email, ask yourself the following questions.

Who is my audience? Defining your audience and understanding what is important to them will help you to create more meaningful content. It will help you decide if one message is appropriate for all or do you need to develop specific messages targeted to different segments of your audience.

What is the purpose of my email campaign and what are the results I want to achieve? Is the purpose of your email campaign to inform, educate, retain customers, get new customers, increase sales, or promote an event? What action do you want your audience to take? By defining your purpose and establishing specific goals you will be able to keep your campaign on track and implement ways to measure the results and gage its success.

How often will I send? Successful email campaigns are consistent. Contact your audience regularly, but don't send just for the sake of sending. Establish a schedule that allows you to provide meaningful content on a regular basis and stick to it.

Have I planned a welcome campaign to engage my new subscribers? An effective welcome campaign will get your relationship with new subscribers off to the right start. It consists of a visible sign up on your website, a subscriber form, a landing page and most importantly, a welcome email that is automatically sent immediately after a new subscriber signs up. Your welcome email is the first impression you will make. It should engage the subscriber and set the expectations and tone for future communications as well as support your bottom-line campaign goals.

How will I measure the results? What metrics you decide to track depends on the purpose of your campaign and your goals. Of course, you will want to know the open rate. The forwarding rate tells you what word-of-mouth marketing you are getting from your newsletter. If you build links into your email, you can track the number of times each link is followed. This is a true indicator that your recipient is interested in your content and a good way to evaluate what is (or is not) working.

2. Detail (Content):

Writing the content at the last moment, or 'making do' because it's time to send, is a one way to ensure the failure of your campaign and to lose subscribers. Map out what you plan to say in each communication in advance. The content of your emails will either motivate your subscribers to keep opening them *or make them unsubscribe.* Keep it relevant and engage your audience. When deciding on your content, ask yourself these questions.

Does my content match the purpose of my email campaign and is it relevant to my target audience? The upfront work you did to when planning your campaign will ensure that when you are writing the content for your emails it tracks with the purpose of your campaign and is relevant to your audience. You defined your audience for this purpose and have segmented your database into specific target groups.

Are my emails personalized? How often do you receive emails with the salutation "Valued Subscriber?" Does it make you feel valued? Don't overlook the power of personalization. We all know that the email we receive is being sent to many recipients, but seeing our name somehow makes it seem more personal.

> *"35% of readers prefer a personalized greeting i.e. 'Hi John'." – Email Marketing eNewsletter Survey*

Is my subject line compelling? Your subject line is the first thing that will determine whether your email is opened, deleted immediately, or reported as spam. Don't be 'tricky' or 'cryptic' with your subject line or it could look like unsolicited email. Keep it short, less than 50 characters is a good rule to follow. It's a good idea to vary your subject lines and to test them in spam filters before sending your email.

Can I provide information to my audience that can be sent automatically? Like most business you have limited time and resources. Being consistent, timely, and relevant can be a challenge. Automating a part of your email campaign can save you time and maximize your content. Automated emails are simply a series of emails that are set up in advance and sent automatically. They can be initiated by an activity, a form or a specific date and can improve the efficiency and effectiveness of your campaign.

How can I make my subscribers feel special? Exclusive email offers, special promotions, and contests can be used to engage your audience and make them feel like they are receiving something special. A personalized eCard greeting is an opportunity to recognize your customers' birthday or a special day. Think about including a gift or a special discount.

3. Design:

While the content of your emails is what is going to keep your subscribers opening your emails, don't overlook the impact the design will have on branding, click-through rates and deliverability. Some questions to ask when designing your email communications include:

Am I using my logo consistently and maximizing my brand identity? As with any marketing campaign, you want to make sure that your email enhances your brand and maintains a consistent look. Your emails should have elements of your website, but not duplicate it. Don't forget to brand your subscriber page and your welcome email. Each piece should be easily recognizable as coming from your company with your unique look.

Do I have a good balance of text and graphics? Use graphics that are relevant to your message. Too many graphics can tag your email as spam. Because most email readers do not automatically download graphics, your message must be communicated clearly even without the graphics. Messages imbedded in graphics may be wasted. Place your most important message and graphics in the top portion of your emails where they will be seen first.

What does my email look like in the preview pane? Don't assume that what you see is what the reader will see when they receive your email. Most email readers have a preview pane; this is most likely this where your readers will get their first look at your email. Is there enough text visible to communicate your message to the reader if your graphics don't download? If you fail to capture your subscriber's interest at this point, they may not even open your message.

How is my email displayed by the major email readers? The way your email is displayed in the many email readers can vary greatly.

So when designing your email template, it is best to keep it simple. For best results, you should test your emails to see how your text and graphics will display in various email readers. This give you an opportunity to correct any design issues before sending out your email.

Have I provided an alternative text version? Giving the subscriber the option of receiving a text version ensures that subscribers who do not wish to receive HTML messages will read your emails.

Is it clear to the reader who the email is from? To be compliant with U.S. spam legislation, ASI (accurate sender information) must be clearly displayed. ASI is your company information, including on-line and off-line contact details.

Have I made the option to subscribe or to unsubscribe clearly visible? An unsubscribe link (an opt-out option) must be on every email. Again, this is to comply with spam legislation. But take advantage of adding new subscribers when your emails *are forwarded* by making sure you also include a link *to subscribe* as well.

4. Database:

The size of your database is not as important as the quality. Fewer, quality contacts will get you more return for your investment. If you're serious about email marketing, make time to update, grow and maintain your database. It will be the basis of your success. Some question to ask when developing your working database.

Am I asking my customers for email addresses? Most customers will happily fill out a form giving you permission to email them on a regular basis. In this age of localization, people want to hear from local businesses.

Do I ask new contacts if they would like to receive my emails? We all know effective networking includes asking everyone you meet for their business card, but you should also ask them if they would like to receive your email communications. Then send a welcome email letting them know they have been subscribed.

Do I have a prominent "sign up" on my website? Make your sign up is appealing and easily found on every page of your website. Promote the benefits of signing up and tell your audience what they will receive.

Do I have a way for my fans and followers on social networks to sign up for my emails? Many businesses promote themselves on social networking sites, but don't take advantage of the opportunity to begin a dialogue with their fans. Have a sign-up for your emails on your social networking page.

> *"More than a third of consumers (36%) said that receiving an email had prompted them to make an online purchase and 27% stated that an email had encouraged them to make an offline investment"*
> *- International Advertising Bureau Survey, 2010.*

Do I have a way to delete unsubscribes from my database and remove bounced emails? Make sure that when someone unsubscribes from your databases *they are removed.* Sending an email to someone who unsubscribes may get you reported as a spammer. Sending repeated emails to bounced addresses may also get you labeled as a spammer, not to mention it is a waste of money.

5. Delivery:

All of the effort you've put into your email marketing campaign is wasted if your email isn't delivered successfully. Test with the major ISPs before each send to make sure your email doesn't trigger any spam filters. Questions to ask before you schedule your email for delivery.

Do I know who the major ISPs are? You are probably familiar with Hotmail, Yahoo, and Gmail, but you should make sure that you test with other ISPs if the majority of your recipients are using them.

What is the size of my email? You might be on super fast broadband but your readers might have a slower Internet connection. So send yourself a test and check the size in your in-box. Preferably, keep your emails and newsletter under 200KB (Kilobytes).

Conclusion:

Understanding the key components of an effective email marketing campaign will help you successfully reach your audience whether you are outsourcing your email marketing or doing it yourself. Email marketing can be very effective way to communicate directly with your customers and potential customers. It is flexible, cost effective, and it can have a positive effect on your bottom line. With the right planning, preparation, testing and tracking, an email campaign is a powerful tool to add to your overall marketing mix.

About the Author: Pamela Cox is an e-mail marketing specialist trained in email marketing best practices. She helps business develop and implement smart email marketing programs that are tailored to complement their level of email marketing experience and the complexity of their email marketing requirements. Her services include planning, custom email design, email testing and delivery, tracking, reporting and analysis. Pamela uses her expertise in email marketing, her 15+ years of experience in sales and marketing, and an advanced email delivery system to create innovative email marketing campaigns that deliver results for her clients.

Contact Info:
Pamela Cox
pamela@pcemailmarketing.com
www.pcemailmarketing.com
831.345.5176, or toll free at 877.742.2786

CHAPTER EIGHTEEN

12 Steps to Creating Money-Making eReports

By Kathleen Gage

We've all heard stories of people making boatloads of money online. There are claims of making hundreds, thousands, and even tens of thousands of dollars in a very short period of time. Is this really possible? Absolutely! Countless numbers of people do this every single day.

Yet, most people will never realize what is possible for a number of reasons. One, they don't have a proven formula for success. Two, they are impatient. Three, they try to make thousands before they make even $100. The fact is before you make thousands, you need to make that first $100. You see, once you make $100, the next $100 is much easier.

One of the best ways to make great money online is by packaging your knowledge. That's right, creating information products in various formats and price points.

What are Information Products?

Information products include books, CDs, MP3s, white papers, reports, teleseminars, webinars, Podcasts, etc. Anything that contains knowledge and can be delivered electronically is considered an electronic information product.

One of the easiest (and quickest) information products to create is a *report*. There are ample benefits to creating low-priced reports. One of the primary benefits is they are easy to sell. Another is they are low risk to the buyer and yet another is they take little time to develop.

You might be wondering why someone would pay for information when just about everything can be accessed for free. Many consumers would rather pay a few dollars for a fast solution to their problem than have to search around for the information (even if it's free).

It doesn't matter what topic, market or industry, reports are a great way to provide solutions to readers and generate great revenue with minimal work.

If you've never developed information products, an eReport is by far you best choice. Benefits to report development are:

- Credibility
- Market reach
- Visibility
- Opt-in subscriber list increase
- Revenues
- Future opportunities

Reports are so easy to create that you can often do so with little or no money out of pocket. Sure, there is time involved, but when you consider that you can generate hundreds (and even thousands) of dollars in revenue from a 10–20 page plus report, the time invested is worth it.

Because your reports will be delivered electronically, there are no storage costs. With physical products you have to keep inventory on hand, find a place to store them and often watch them collect dust. This won't happen with online reports.

After the initial costs of developing your report, there are literally no additional costs to continue selling them. That is unless you have an affiliate program set up. Then you pay your affiliates based on performance.

The following 12 steps explain exactly what you need to do to be well on your way to making money with reports.

1. Determine what your market needs, wants, and *is willing to pay for.*

Before you write your first word, you need to know who you are writing for. Far too often someone will develop an information product before they have clearly defined who they are writing for, what the problem is for those they are writing for, and what the solution is.

Identifying your market is an ongoing process. Who your market is today may not be who they are a year from now. As you grow and change, so does your market.

Also consider...

- Who will buy your product?

- Is there a primary or secondary target market?

- Is there a big enough market for your products?

- What factors influence their decision to buy?

- Who is involved in the purchase decision?

- How often will they buy?

- Where do they currently buy, when and how much?

- Is there opportunity to turn casual buyers into loyal buyers?

- Can you build a long-term relationship with your market?

2. Identify the problem

It's amazing how many people will develop information products before they even know if there is a problem and desire for their solution. Some people have spent hundreds of hours and thousands of dollars, and have expended tons of energy, developing very complex offerings only to find out what they thought the market wanted is *not at all what they wanted.*

Low-cost reports are one of the most cost-effective ways to see how your market will respond to solutions you offer. If there is not an interest from your market for a low-priced report *how do you expect to sell a high priced program or offering to them?*

Developing a low-priced report will give you a good indication if people are interested in what you are providing a solution for.

And not only can you make money with the report, you can learn a lot about what your market wants this way.

It's actually quite easy to identify the problem a specific market has.

- **Survey potential buyers.** Develop a short, simple and easy to answer survey by utilizing free services on the Internet. One of my favorites for this is Survey Monkey at www.survey-monkey.com

- **Visit online forums geared to your market**. To find forums do a Google search specific to your market. For example, if you train Boxer dogs input "Boxer Dogs + Forums." This will bring up some great resources to do your research in.

- **Notice what your clients are asking for.** Paying attention to your client needs is an ongoing process.

- **Surf social networks.** Social networks such as Facebook and LinkedIn are yet another way to find out what people need. As with forums you can learn a great deal simply by observing.

- **Read or create a micro blog**. Micro blogs such as Twitter are yet another way to find out what people are "buzzing" about.

- **Pay attention to what's happening in media**. Are there specific trends occurring? When the economy took a dip, there was ample opportunity for experts in the finance, home buying, mortgage lending, stress management, life balance and job search industries to develop great low priced reports. Simply by paying attention to what was being written and talked about in traditional media gave experts ample information to know where the market's pain point was.

3. Create a Title

Your title is one of the most important parts of your report. You don't want to take this aspect of your report development lightly. The title and subtitle can make or break the success of your report. People often make their buying decisions on how "catchy" a title is.

Keep your title specific to your market. Rather than, "Everything you want to know about dogs," try, "The selection and care of _____ dogs." You could fill it in with just about any breed.

Granted, you may target owners of all types of dog breeds, but chances are each report you write will address a specific area.

Think of it this way; if you put everything in your first report you'll miss opportunities for other reports for the same market.

Some great words that have worked for me in some of my information products are

• How to

• Secrets of

• 101 Ways to

A few of the best words to use are free, guaranteed, how to, secret and discover. Of course there are many more but these are words that consistently produce results.

4. Develop a Series of 10 – 15 Solutions Regarding the Problem

Once you have identified what keeps your market "awake at night," outline solutions to the problem. Write the solutions in bullet format. Develop one to three paragraphs for each bullet point.

Initially, don't worry about the writing being perfect. Your goal should be to get the information out. You, or an editor, can edit later.

5. Record the Problem and the Solutions

If writing is not your favorite thing to do you can actually record your answers and have the recording transcribed. This will likely cost a bit more but for many experts this is a great solution.

6. Edit

With either the transcripts or what you wrote, you need to edit and clean up as needed. You may want to consider the services of a virtual assistant who specializes in editing.

7. Format

When the editing is complete you need to format your document using Word or something comparable. Add in the title, disclaimer page, header and footer, page numbers, subheads and graphics as needed.

8. Convert to a PDF file

Once you have completed all of the above steps, you need to convert your information product into a format that is universally recognized. Adobe Acrobat is a great solution for converting a document into a PDF. You can add in live links such as your blog or web address, affiliate links for products you mention in your report, and links to support a point you are making in your report. Plus, providing your report in a PDF file protects the content from being easily edited or copied by the recipient.

9. Decide on a Price

Reports can range in price from $5 up to $37 plus. The price points I have found work well are $7 and $9 for short (under 15 pages) reports, $17 for longer reports like this one and upwards of $37 if you are creating a massive amount of value.

Pricing also depends on your level of expertise, how much the market views you as an expert, what else is available to your potential buyers and the industry. You will likely not be able to charge as much for something being sold to low to moderate income people as you would to six figure professionals.

Test pricing, titles, subjects and sales copy. The more you do this the closer you get, but no matter how long you do this you will have times you absolutely need to test.

10. Develop the landing/sales page

A landing page is your 24/7 sales tool. Just like a live salesperson, it has to address any questions, concerns and/or objections a buyer might have. The main elements of your landing page are:

- Headline
- Copy
- Images
- Benefit statements
- Opt in box

Your goal with a landing page/squeeze page should be for visitors to quickly see what they are looking for. Whether it is to get a visitor to click, buy, register for something or tell a friend about your site/services, optimizing your landing pages is essential to a successful report launch.

11. Follow-up with Autoresponders

Create a series of emails to promote the landing page and report. A mistake many people new to product sales make is not being proactive enough with their email marketing. It takes more than one message for some buyers to take action.

12. Market Your Report

An area many people neglect to give 100% to is the marketing. The fact is, you can have the greatest report in the world, but if potential buyers don't know about it you won't make money.

Here are some very effective ways to market your report: Email your opt-in subscriber list; put the link to it in your email signature file; write a press release about it, write articles with a link back to the landing page of the report; run solo and classified online advertisements; and promote it through Social Media marketing, blogging, guest blogging, your own online newsletter, testimonials and affiliate partnerships.

So there you have it—the formula for creating, marketing and selling eReports! Use this formula for just about any information product you take to market and you will be amazed at the possibilities.

About the Author: Kathleen Gage is the Founder of The Street Smarts Marketing System, and is an Internet marketing advisor who works with spiritually aware speakers, authors, coaches and consultants who are ready to turn their information into money making products and services. And as an award-winning speaker, author and entrepreneur, Kathleen is best known for her expertise with teleseminars, online bestseller book launches, information product development and continuity programs. She is committed to helping others discover how their life's work and spiritual path go hand in hand.

Contact Info:
www.kathleengage.com
www.thestreetsmartsmarketer.com
http://www.facebook.com/KathleenGage
http://www.linkedin.com/in/kathleengage
http://twitter.com/kathleengage

CHAPTER NINETEEN

30 Hot Tips on How to Become a Blogtalk Radio Rock Star

By Vicki Flaugher

Blogtalk Radio is an Internet radio network that lets you create and host your own radio show. All you really need is a phone, although having a computer to manage your account and live show panel is highly preferred and recommended. A basic account is free and affordable, but premium paid accounts with additional features are available as well. It's a fun, easy way to extend your brand and image into the marketplace.

One of the great benefits of Blogtalk is that it is wide open. Unlike regular broadcast radio, you do not have to be rich or famous enough to talk someone into booking your show. You do not have to go to a production studio during certain limited hours. You are not restricted to topics that only a large "drive time" audience wants to hear. You can talk about whatever you like, including specialty topics where a smaller base of passionate fans exists. And, you can do it today, right now, for free, without any of the typical cost and content restrictions that come with soliciting and pleasing sponsors.

Another benefit is that Blogtalk shows are recorded, archived and published out to iTunes. You can (and should!) place the Blogtalk Radio show badge on your website. Since you retain the copyright for the shows, you can even use the recordings to create information products. The potential is limited only by your imagination.

Blogtalk shows typically rank high in search engines like Google, which is a huge marketing advantage. More mentions on Google featuring your expertise will garner you targeted attention and is an effective way to build a fan base. Add in the rapport and trust factor of letting your potential fans get to know you through your show, and you are one huge step ahead of other people who aren't willing to put themselves out there. It really does pay to step up and step out.

As a side note, Blogtalk Radio is more than just a promotional broadcast opportunity…it's a social network. Thousands of people visit Blogtalkradio.com every day and many of the hosts and listeners interact. It's perfect for socializing, so relationships are easy to cultivate and nurture. It's like one big 24/7 radio show party, so put on your party attitude and let's go!

Here are 30 hot tips to become a Blogtalk Radio rock star:

1. Act professionally and be prepared for your show. Start your show on time and end it on time.

2. For best audio quality, buy a **decent microphone headset** (if you call in via Skype) or use your landline phone rather than your cell phone to call in.

3. Find a place that is quiet for your broadcast and do your best to feel relaxed and ready. External noises and distractions will affect your ability to be "on" so eliminate them the best you can. Your show is essentially a performance and it needs and deserves your full attention.

4. Think about the **topic** you've selected ahead of time, make some bullet point notes, and stay on track. Your show will likely be a blend of entertainment and information so concentrate on the experience you want to deliver to your listeners.

5. Even if your show is homey and casual in its style, you are playing the role of a journalist as the host. Think about what it is that makes a radio show host whom you admire so likeable and listenable. From this, you have a good roadmap for how to act.

6. Think about your audience and **pick a broadcast time that makes sense for your audience**. Some of the more popular free account schedule times might be taken, so you won't always get your #1 preference, but do your best.

7. If live scheduling is an issue, a premium account allows you to **upload pre-recorded files** at any time. If that better fits your lifestyle, you can choose that.

8. The audience who listens to the *recorded archives* often ends up being four to ten times larger than the live show broadcast audience. So don't worry if no one shows up to listen live. Act like there are a thousand people there regardless…because with archives, there might be.

9. Create good content and your audience will grow over time.

10. Act as your audience's mouthpiece during your show. If you have a guest on who is claiming something that you know your audience would not agree with, speak up.

11. You are the surrogate for your audience and you represent their voice. It's your responsibility to ensure the show is understandable and accessible.

12. Put on some glitz—find some great music and use it to jazz up your intros and exits. If you know a musician or a songwriter who can create a custom piece for you, that would be fantastic.

13. The BlogTalk Radio's main website has links to several sources of podcast free audio you are allowed to use. Find something that captures the spirit of your show and dress up your presentation with music.

14. To edit your music clips into shorter lengths and add sound effects and voiceovers, you can use a free audio program called Audacity. It works much like a cut-n-paste word processor and can be lots of fun to use.

15. Upload any mp3 files to your show panel with sufficient time ahead of your show start so the system has enough time to upload it fully and have the file available. When your show starts, all you have to do is click play on the file and it will trigger.

16. Generally speaking, 15- and 30-minute promo and voiceover spots are best. Launch one at the show intro before you begin talking, one each at 15 minute intervals, and finally, an exit piece as you close the show.

17. There are very strict laws about using copyrighted materials, and your show won't be a very good promotional tool if you get shut down for violating the Terms and Conditions of Blogtalk. Don't do it.

18. Although Blogtalk does not allow explicit paid advertisements, remember that you are promoting yourself. Mention your call-in number, give your name, highlight the day's topic, and invite listeners to participate.

19. Model your behavior off of traditional radio slots and work in a station ID at appropriate times. You don't need to overdo it; aim for a mention once every fifteen minutes.

20. Send listeners to your website address, encourage them to sign up for your newsletter, and ask them follow you on Social Media.

21. If you have a guest, ask them to submit a promo spot that you can play like a commercial.

22. Other marketing tools for you to leverage are your host bio, your show description, your avatar, show keyword tags and the onsite blog available on your radio show page. Use concise and descriptive words that relate to your brand and to what your show is about.

23. Link up your show publishing to your Social Media via the automated tools on the site.

24. Add links from the onsite blog at Blogtalk to your external website that continues the conversation or offers a promotional eBook or newsletter signup.

25. As with any online promotion, remember that you're in public. You should not act like you are at home alone, even though you might actually *be* at home alone. Your show will remain as a permanent record that future clients and employers can access. Be smart about it.

26. More voices are better than just one. Use a co-host, a side-kick, or featured interview guests (or all of these combined). It makes for a more interesting show.

27. One advantage of a co-host or a sidekick is that they can fill in when you are sick or not available. They can add their voice and also help by firing off the promo spots, keeping you on time, queuing up the call-in guests, and moderating the chat room. And an extra pair of hands can manage the small bit of technical require-ments more easily, especially when you are hosting multiple guests in one show or have a very active chat room.

28. Having featured guests can get you a wider promotional reach. They will likely tell their fan base about you and are equally likely to post your show badge on their blog. Most people feel honored to be featured and are delighted to participate.

29. Blogtalk Radio allows only five call-in lines active at any one time, but an unlimited number of people can show up in your online chat room. So be sure to highlight the conversations there to add an interesting dimension to your show when you're flying solo.

30. Ahead of the show, send less media savvy guests tips on how to be a good guest, as well as a list of questions to guide the inter-view. Tell them the promo spot schedule so they are more likely to quit talking when you want to go to break. Set the expectation that they are to dialogue with you rather than monologue like a presen-tation. A reminder email a day or two before the scheduled interview time is a good idea too.

Blogtalk Radio can be a highly leveraged, effective marketing tool for promoting yourself and your business or cause. Some of your best future opportunities will come from your guests and their network so reach out and ask your mentors or colleagues to be on your show. It's those relationships as well as the ones that you develop through your listeners that will pay you dividends. You can connect with like minds and new audiences, have compelling conversations, and position yourself as an expert. Put these tips to good use, be yourself, and let your personality shine. Best of success and have fun with it!

About the Author: Vicki Flaugher, aka @SmartWoman, has been an online marketing strategist for 10 years, helping her clients become famous in their niche by crafting compelling online personas. She's been recognized in Forbes as one of 30 Women Entrepreneurs to Follow on Twitter, as well as one of WE Magazine's Bloggers to Watch. Her personal passionate purpose is helping to empower female entrepreneurs worldwide through education, micro-lending, and market access. To download free tools and resources to help you leverage Blogtalk Radio better in your business, sign up here: http://bit.ly/PromoteUGuru_blogtalk

Contact Info:
Vicki Flaugher, CEO
512-917-3347
vicki@smartwomanpublishing.com
Website http://SmartWomanGuides.com
Linked In http://linkedin.com/in/smartwoman
Twitter http://twitter.com/smartwoman
Facebook http://facebook.com/vickiflaugher
Blogtalk Radio Show http://budurl.com/radioshow
Speaking Samples http://www.talkshoe.com/tc/66283

CHAPTER TWENTY

Ten Essentials for Making YOU A
Sales Success with Happiness and Heart

By Diane Marie Pinkard

Somehow, consumers just know when they have landed with the qualified professional they have been searching for. They sense your genuine value of integrity; they pick up on your poise, your self-confidence, and your sincere interest in them. They know when they have found the right person to fulfill their needs. They know when they have found the person they want to work with. In other words, they recognize that you are there for them, and not yourself, and that *you are a "keeper."*

Today, our world feels like it is gyrating out of control. Life has become very hectic, very chaotic. People have a lot going on in their lives, and many are feeling extremely time-pressed and anxious. When they have major purchases and important decisions to make, they become even more overwhelmed. They are subjected to information overload about product quality or performance, all the choices of products to select from, and the multitude of sources to buy from.

Customers in this stressed and frustrated state are desperate for proficient sales professionals who will take charge and help them complete their purchasing needs. Customers yearn for the process to be simple. Secretly, they are searching for someone to simply take their hand and offer them "a safe place to land." They yearn to be in a place where they are comfortable as they work their way through the sometimes complicated buying experience.

They long to find someone they can trust—someone who is honest, a good listener, and genuinely cares enough to assist them. If they don't find that person, something will trigger inside of them, they will get frustrated, and they will walk out the door, or leave a website, *and be gone.*

So, let's look at some simple, user-friendly ways to make *you* a "keeper," so you can explode *your* selling success:

1. The first person you have to learn to sell to is you! Before selling successfully to the world, you must learn to sell successfully to yourself. This means learning to identify with your own character and makeup; it means getting in touch with your own personal truth. I define *my* personal truth to be what I say to myself when no one else is listening. By experimenting with this process, you too will discover your own personal truth. This is a great way to discover your own touch of greatness—the "real makings of you."

Find your authentic self. Whatever you do in life, don't envy or try mimicking someone else. Discover your own touch of greatness. Then unveil this hidden secret to the world. Believe that everything you need is within you, because it is.

2. "People buy from people, and they buy the most from people that treat them like they matter." This simple, cheerful proclamation is the heart and soul of all my teaching I bring to you. Successful selling is not only about closing the sale, it's about building quality relationships, rich connections, and loyal trust—first with yourself, and then with your customers.

3. If personal growth intrigues and excites you, then learning about sales is the best experience you can have for achieving your goals. See yourself as being in the business of human resource development. Delving in and learning more about yourself will better align you with your own human spirit. The more self-awareness you possess, the easier it will be for you to connect with others and the more savvy you will become about the complexities of human nature. The more knowledgeable you become, the less you will allow yourself to be offended by others who may have hidden agendas or wish to see you fail. You'll be able to recognize that their behavior is about them, not about you. Embarking on a journey of personal growth will greatly improve your ability to intuitively relate to others in a good way, and also to sell.

Yes, your personal growth and professional growth travel hand in hand! Learning sales will give you the opportunity to challenge yourself and learn freedom of expression so you can better communicate and connect in a very satisfying manner. Sales professionals are not born—they are developed and transformed because of their passion for people and their love and curiosity about human nature. They possess a personal drive to teach and train themselves. Salespeople are eagerly searching for their empowered presence. They have the desire to invest a lot of time and effort into their own evolution. And there's no better investment than investing time in yourself and your personal development.

4. Overcome your greatest obstacle—yourself! Listen to what you're saying to yourself! Are you your own worst enemy? Are you negative, defensive, or critical? Are you just plain self-defeating, manipulative, and relentless in relating all the reasons why you can't achieve success? If so, take a personal inventory and if you do not like what you see, get the help you need to re-program the personal tapes you are playing to yourself.

5. Don't wait until you feel better about yourself or believe you have what it takes to finally achieve success. Instead, be self-actualized and your new positive beliefs will automatically follow suit. Move forward even if you are afraid. Don't wait until you are not. Otherwise, one of two things will happen—or worse yet, both. First, you can be sure the day will never come when you finally feel better about yourself. Second, you may never overcome all of your fears. Welcome your fears; view them as a stimulating wake-up call to broaden your horizons.

6. As a sales professional see yourself like a talented artist. When you perform to your highest ability, your steps transcend that of a beautifully choreographed dance. Your graceful moves harmonize with the natural flow of human nature, and echo what the universe so badly wants and needs. The process of facilitating life is, quite simply, dancing to the heartbeat and soul of humanity. And there is no better place to practice these moves than to walk out to center stage…on the virtual or live sales floor.

7. Discover the simple secrets for being charismatic. Have you had others say to you, "Wow, you just know how to bring out the best in people." "I'm not used to feeling so happy (so nice, so fun or whatever), as I do when I am around you." "Being in your company just seems to bring out the best in me."

Can you imagine what the world would be like if each and every one of us discovered the simple secret of this true "charismatic power?" Wrongly, our culture teaches us that being charismatic is about drawing, even inspiring and charming, the attention of others towards ourselves. This may involve grandiose gestures, good looks and style, dramatic actions, and endearing and manipulative characteristics.

But, being charismatic is _not_ about deliberately drawing attention to ourselves. Rather, it is about *you* showering your attention completely on the value and worth of *others*. It is about you asking lots of good questions and listening intently to their answers and responses. By focusing your *undivided* attention in this sincere manner, indirectly and effortlessly, you capture the attention of everyone around you. People feel like they matter when they are *treated like they matter.* It is just that basic!

8. You will be remembered for sharing a quality conversation. We are all so busy talking, but is anyone really having a conversation? Is anybody really listening? Everywhere you turn these days, someone is talking on a cell phone—in a car, in the store, on the street. Everyone is hooked up and plugged in with electronic gear, creating tons of noise pollution. Everywhere we turn, there is so much noise, so much commotion, so much stimulus, for adults and kids alike. Life feels chaotic!

When we fill every waking moment with external stimulation, leaving little time for quiet reflection, we grow distant from the most important relationship we have—the one we have with ourselves. Overstimulation not only quells our thought process, it also contributes to a fractional quality in our lives. As a result, we function as poor listeners and poor conversationalists. Both listening and conversing are dying arts in our overwhelmed society today. Hello? Is anybody even listening?

Good conversation is valuable for so many reasons: It enables us to connect to our prospects and clients, our professional contacts, our friends, and our family, not to mention strangers. Good conversational skills make people want to respond to you and make things happen, so things get done. Rich sharing so graciously soothes the soul and warms the heart. Stimulating conversation brings people alive to interrelate in the here and now, enhancing the quality for enjoying the moment.

Quality conversation requires a few active ingredients; prerequisites are time and willing, thoughtful participants. The design is to blend all of the participants' ideas and thoughts so everyone feels heard and valued. Being understood yourself, and understanding others, serves to strengthen our hope for mankind. It's a beautiful practice of "Give and Take."

9. We all love to feel comfortable! Joe Navarro, author of *Louder Than Words,* educates us about experiencing comfort and discomfort—that at all times we are feeling one or the other. He teaches us how to be able to read the non-verbal signals that represent comfort or discomfort. He emphasizes that the significance of this knowledge is conducive for nurturing business prospects and clients, and effective selling. He also states that being able to recognize the comfort/discomfort paradigm is an indispensible tool for everyday business…and it's free! I highly suggest you pick up a copy of Joe's book as it is a must-read for anyone in business.

10. Master the desire, the passion, and the ability to reach out to people with compassion. Nothing compares to the wonderful, welcoming sensations we have when we sense that someone really understands and cares about us. To quote Bruce Springsteen, "Everybody has a hungry heart." Humans thrive on healthy interpersonal connections. We are meant to be happy, social creatures. And it's so easy to achieve this bond by kindly extending a personal part of ourselves to others.

Today, we are living on the fast track in a rapidly changing world. Due to our modern existence, smothered with automation and highly sophisticated technology, making contact with a truly caring and competent service specialist is becoming more and more of a rarity. In our time-pressed society, we are all so busy multi-tasking that we have lost touch with the precious aptitude for human caring and enjoyable interconnectedness with one another.

So what can you do to make a worthwhile contribution and difference in our spinning, out-of-control world? Be different from other "salespeople" simply by slowing down your tempo. Take that extra moment to treat your new prospects as though they are someone special…because they are! Take a few moments to tap into them; ask them about themselves and their talents, and listen to their responses with genuine interest. Let them know you are there *with* them and *for* them. Treat them the way you would like to be treated! You will be truly amazed with the wondrous results—your efforts will pay off tenfold!

I realize that not everyone is nice and/or receptive, nor do they want to be, and that's just how the ball bounces. But what in the world do you have to lose by graciously channeling yourself to this euphoric place and seeing where it takes you? Again, this effort costs you nothing. It's free! It seems almost impossible for me to express in words the blissful feelings you will experience when you realize the beautiful contribution you are gifting to others.

Besides the joy you are giving others, look at the wealth of goodness that you are flooding into your own soul. Your sunshine energy not only affects your recipient, it permeates our universe. Think of your actions as a much-needed, healthy new epidemic—your vibrant, radiant behavior will catch on and become contagious. It's really that simple!

Now, more than ever you need to dig deeper and tune in into your own meta-communication skills and non-verbal intelligence, to be better able to read your prospects and customers. You need to align yourself with the healthy gut feeling that your clients are either, consciously or unconsciously, searching for...*so you can be a "keeper."*

About the Author: Diane Marie Pinkard is a 40-year sales expert, sales trainer, and the author of the award winning book, *Just Treat Me Like I Matter: The Heart of Sales*. With her creative and unique approach to sales training she was a finalist in the 2009 Stevie Awards for "Creative Professional of the Year." And her training is based upon her methodology of "Sales Success with Happiness and Heart." Diane has launched and operated three successful businesses and has earned the reputation of being an accomplished professional in a number of sales arenas. She is available for sales training, speaking, and mentoring upon request.

Contact Info:
Diane Marie Pinkard
"Sales Success with Happiness and Heart"
Sales Trainer – Sales Consultant – Sales Coach and Mentor
1.866.552.2510 (toll free)
info@HeartofSales.com
www.HeartofSales.com
Twitter @HeartofSales
Facebook: HeartofSales
LinkedIn: Diane Marie Pinkard

CHAPTER TWENTY-ONE

Writing Articles to Build Your Brand & Website Traffic

By Lisa Orrell

A very powerful strategy for *building* your topic expert brand positioning, as well as for *driving traffic* to your website, is to write articles and submit them to online article distribution services. Some people also choose to do this for additional income because there are some article services and media outlets that will pay for your articles. But many experts don't do it for pay; they write articles for the two key reasons I mentioned in the first sentence

In this chapter, I'd like to outline 12 ways to make your articles compelling so that they become significant traffic generators for your website. I'll then conclude this chapter by providing a list of some popular online article submission and distribution services that you can use to get your articles read by the masses.

12 Ways to Create Articles for Brand Building:

When you write interesting articles in your area of expertise, it can quickly position you as *an expert in your field.* It also gives you the opportunity to showcase your knowledge and this can attract clients to you, as well as attract media interviews for you. And if you're not a great writer, don't panic! You can hire ghostwriters (inexpensively) who will write them for you. All you need to do is provide them with the topics you think will benefit your target audience.

However, regardless of whether you write the articles or someone does it for you, here are 12 tips for making them compelling and valuable marketing tools for you:

1. Grab the Reader's Attention Fast: Make sure to create an interesting title for your article; you can even make it <u>a thought-provoking question</u>. Also, in your opening paragraph set-up the "pain point" you're going to solve and why it's important to them. Writing articles that will *solve a problem for your target audience* is a great strategy for the topic angles you develop.

2. Keep the Articles Simple and Easy to Understand Quickly: People want to read quick-hit information that they can grasp fast and benefit from. So make sure the articles you write provide genuinely valuable, helpful information and are written in a succinct style. A good way to achieve this is to use <u>bullet points or numbered points</u> so that your key messages and tips are easy to reference and follow. Having your key points "buried" in paragraphs will make it frustrating for your readers, so you might want to use sub-headings to help set the stage

3. Add Keywords for Online Search Engine Optimization: Your articles will be posted in numerous ways online and will often be found by people doing keyword searches on your topic matter. Therefore, you want to make sure that you use the Google keyword tool that I mentioned back in the chapter about writing an effective press release, and <u>add those popular search terms in the body of your articles</u>. I know many experts who rapidly increase their search engine rankings because of writing articles, and oftentimes their articles start ranking higher in search results than their main websites do. Therefore, you want to implement this strategy!

4. Make Your Articles Short: An article doesn't have to be super-long to be super-good. This is about quality not quantity! Most articles that I, and other experts write, are around <u>400-700 words</u>. Keeping them short not only makes it easier for your readers, it also makes it easier for <u>you</u> to write them on an on-going basis. And let's face it: What's 'easy' is more likely to get done, right?

5. Don't Pitch Your Services and Products: Your only goal when you write articles is to provide helpful info to your target audience. It is *not* about making your articles big infomercials that pitch yourself and/or your products. If you write good articles that people truly benefit from, they will typically want to learn more about you and they will visit your website. The fastest way to kill your credibility and lose a potential "fan or client" is by trying to overtly sell them on something in your article content.

6. Be Yourself in Your Writing Style: Conveying yourself as *authentic* is important! If you're a lighthearted, fun-loving individual, be sure to bring out your personality in your articles; if you're a serious, thoughtful person, write in a way that reflects that attribute. This is the same advice I give to clients who are embarking on their speaking careers! Don't be one person on the stage and another person off stage. People can see through that because you're not being authentic. And when you write articles, it may be the FIRST contact anyone has with you; even before seeing your website. So you want to make sure *who you really are* comes through in your writing. Even if you're using a ghostwriter, that person should write in your 'voice.' A good example of this is my own writing style. As you know from reading this book, I write in an informal, conversational, way, and it's very close to how I speak with people. I'm not afraid to add in sarcastic comments, casual verbiage or silly phrases to anything I write because that's who I am…and I want my readers to get to know the 'real Lisa,' not a manufactured version.

7. Don't Quote Other Experts: The purpose of your articles is to showcase *you;* not someone who could be a competitor. You normally only want to quote other people in your articles if their information really adds to your message and content quality. The exception would be quoting stats and research results from studies you find; just try to avoid quoting or mentioning other experts who are similar to you.

8. Offer Your Articles on Your Website: When I submit articles online, I also add them to my website, in Word, so that people can download them to use as content on their own blogs, e-zines, websites and newsletters. Millions of people are constantly on the prowl for content and understand they have to source the author who wrote it. So, on my article web page, I clearly state they can use my articles as long as they are shown in their entirety and the short bio about me provided at the end of each article is included. I also ask that they send me a link to it when it's used. (I don't mind sharing my content for free, but getting credit for what I've written is non-negotiable.) This strategy is great for driving *their* traffic to *me*. It will do the same for you.

9. Create an E-book: Once you have several articles done, you can leverage the value of that content and compile them into an e-book to offer as a free gift on your website (as long as people provide you with their contact info to download it), or as a for-sale item. Either way, this is a good strategy for creating simple products and for building your contact list.

10. Write and Submit Consistently: If possible, try to write and submit at least one article per month online. I know experts who do one-per-week because they receive so much benefit from doing so, but that may be tough for many of you. Start by writing a few, and after you get the hang of it and start developing a "formula" for cranking them out (or hire a ghostwriter to do them for you), you can start to increase how many you produce monthly. And there's no law against writing your articles in advance so that they're ready to go even when you're ultra-busy. Just make sure the information is up to date.

11. Share Your Links: Many article distribution services will create a web page for your article that will be found through online searches. You'll have a unique url for your article's page and can share that link to drive traffic to your article by posting it on Twitter, Facebook, LinkedIn, in blog comments, and in emails to your contact database.

12. Embed Links in Your Articles: When you write an article, make sure to have certain words or phrases that have hyperlinks to pages on your website, your blog posts, Twitter page, Facebook page, and/or to other articles you have written and that are posted online. Just make sure the links take them to info that is relevant to what you're writing about and to points you are making. And, because links contribute to your online visibility and search engine ranking, this is an important step to implement.

Online Article Submission & Distribution Services:

Okay! So, you've outlined a list of article topics your target audience will benefit from, and you've written your first article. Now what? There are a wide variety of online article submission and distribution services available that operate in different ways and that serve different purposes.

Here is a brief overview of the types that you'll encounter. Distribution services may or may not require you to pay a minimal fee, to distribute your article online and create a web page for your article that can be found in search results. Or, they will have subscribers who pay a monthly fee to access fresh content (i.e. articles submitted by experts like you) and those people will use your article in their blogs, e-zines, websites, publications or newsletters. Or, the service will pay *you* a minimal fee if they approve your article and choose to offer it on their website for others to publish. Or, they will charge you a minimal fee to distribute your articles to *targeted* outlets interested in your topic matter (rather than just distribute it randomly online).

You can find examples of services that match the variety of alternatives I just provided by performing online searches using phrases like: Free services to submit articles; online article submission; getting paid to write or submit articles; and services to distribute articles online. I will mention, however, that at the time of my writing this, Google has some new rules coming out about "repetitive" content that could change how and where online articles should be distributed. So perform a quick Google search to get any up-dated info about this before you run to the services I list below.

That said, as of right now, you will quickly see there are hundreds of options to get your article distributed and found by your target audience! It can be a bit overwhelming, so start by picking a few and try them out.

Another option, if you have the budget, is to hire a VA (Virtual Assistant) or a **freelance article submission expert**, and they can do all of this for you. You can find people who can help you by posting a request on a service like eLance.com and you'll receive responses from many individuals who offer this type of support. Plus, you can also find article ghostwriters on eLance.com who are reasonably priced! Better yet, some freelancers do both.

But, if you plan to get your articles out to the masses by your-self, here is a short list of 10 popular resources to check out. At the time of this writing, they were all still active services:

1. Ezinearticles.com
2. Amazines.com
3. ArticleCity.com
4. WebArticles.com
5. ArticlesFactory.com
6. ArticleFinders.com
7. Content-Articles.com
8. BlogCarnival.com
9. ArticleCube.com
10. GoArticles.com

Before I conclude this chapter, I'd like to share one more strategy you can implement for getting your articles distributed: Contact publications and blogs *directly* that reach your target audi-ence. No matter what your area of expertise is, there are going to be tons of magazines, e-zines, newsletters (print and online), websites, Social Media community websites, and blogs *seeking content from outside experts just like you.*

You can do online searches to find the ones who reach your target audience and then **create a targeted hit-list** to inquire if they accept guest articles. You will find that some of them will even have article submission guidelines available on their websites!

If they find your topic ideas interesting, *feel their audience will benefit* from your information, and find your articles to be well-written, there's a very good chance they will publish your content.

And, even better, you will begin to establish a relationship with these targeted contacts and that can lead to their accepting your articles on a regular basis. This is a fabulous scenario because *their audience* will become more familiar *with you* and that is a key factor for building your topic expert brand!

CHAPTER TWENTY-TWO

How You Can Get Corporate Sponsors for More Income

By Linda Hollander

As topic experts and speakers, we are always looking for creative ways to generate revenue outside of simply speaking and consulting. A great way is with corporate sponsors.

A sponsor can help you do what *you* love, while *they* foot the bill. It's a great way for you to get resources to run your business, reach more people, and make more money.

I'm just like you (or who you aspire to be!). I'm a speaker and skills trainer that does local and nationwide speaking, delivering life-changing messages to audiences virtually and at live events. I've worked with many top tier sponsors such as Citibank, Fed Ex, American Airlines, Staples, Marriott Vacation Club, Hansen's Beverage, Wal-Mart and IBM.

I speak to women business owners and am the founder of the Annual Women's Small Business Expo, a live event in Los Angeles. When I needed more revenue for my speaking and consulting business, I started looking toward corporate sponsors and found that they were willing to give me money. And, with sponsor dollars, I didn't need to pay the money back, so there was no debt!

Here's How Sponsorship Works:

You target companies based on the demographics you reach and what benefits you can offer. Call the prospective sponsors and send them a sponsorship proposal with the description of the people you speak to, marketing plan, benefits, mission statement and the sponsor fees. Follow up with your prospective sponsors, finalize the agreement, and collect the sponsor fee. Then repeat the process again for yearly renewals.

Definition of Sponsorship:

Let's start with the definition of sponsorship: It's a fee paid to a property (aka: person or business entity) in return for access to the commercial potential associated with *that property.*

Your speaking business is your "property" in the sponsor world. Think about Rachael Ray. She is a *property* and one of her sponsors (at the time of this writing) is Nabisco.

Sponsor fees can be *cash or in-kind.* In-kind sponsorships (also called trade sponsorships or soft dollars) are a trading of benefits and services. We all need cash to run our speaking businesses, but in-kind sponsorships can be extremely valuable, too. The biggest in-kind sponsorships are with the media. I've received $25,000 in value just from one radio station in a sponsorship deal and they brought lots of people to my speaking event. In-kind sponsorships can also be leveraged to get cash sponsors. Media gives you extended reach to more people, which in turn, can attract cash sponsors to you.

6 Benefits of Having Corporate Sponsors

1. Increased Income - As speakers and entrepreneurs, you often ride the business roller coaster. You get speaking opportunities and clients. Life is good. But then business gets slow and the bills keep on coming. You need to scramble to get more speaking opportunities. If you know that your sponsor fees will be coming on a continual basis, this revenue lets you play at a higher level. You can even achieve "celebrity" status (even if it's just in a specific industry versus "mainstream"), reach more people, and dream even bigger.

2. Credibility and Expert Status - Being sponsored by leading-edge companies bestows you with more credibility. People see that first-rate sponsors are entrusting *you with their brand image.* This gives you more authority in the marketplace.

3. More Clients - There is a simple rule in business: if you want to be successful, hang out with successful people. Having sponsors helps you get more clients and referrals.

4. Mass Exposure - Sponsors also help promote you to their colleagues, employees, and their customers.

5. Annual Sponsorship Renewals - After you get your sponsors you can get annual renewals again and again. I recommend a 1-year contract with a 1-year renewal. Sponsorship is a relationship business, so keep in touch with your sponsors all year. Then you'll be more successful with renewals.

6. The Ability to Help More People - As a topic expert and speaker, and you're also in the life-changing business. Sponsorship gives you the resources to grow your speaking business, help more people and change more lives.

8 Tips on Getting Corporate Sponsors:

1. Remember That It's About the Sponsor, Not about You - One of the biggest mistakes sponsor-seekers make is that they wax rhapsodic about their business, but don't talk how they can benefit their sponsor. Sponsors want to know that you understand their company, marketing campaigns, goals and visions. You can learn this in your initial conversation with the sponsor, or on the sponsor's website. And if your prospective sponsor is a public company, you can order their Annual Report. Plus, when you talk to the sponsor, remember to ask them *about their goals first*, then go into your presentation and tell them how you can help them accomplish their goals.

2. Be Clear About Your Demographics - Most topic experts and speakers have been trained to think of their message as the most important thing. In the world of corporate sponsorships, your demographic (also called the target audience) is one of the most valuable assets that you can offer a corporate sponsor. There are various ways to research your demographic. You can do an Internet search for statistics on your target demographic. Your demographic reads certain publications, so you can *order the media kit for these publications* and get some great statistics about your demographic.

3. Have a Great Platform - Sponsors want to know that you have extended reach to people who buy things (think Oprah). These could be your clients, people on your email list, your company database, your advisory board and your strategic alliances. Remember if you don't have extended reach to lots of people, then other people do. Use the powerful strategies of borrowed credibility, media and joint ventures.

4. Have Cause-Related Marketing Opportunities - Cause-related marketing is a sales or promotional partnership between the sponsor and a property helping the community. People buy more from companies that give back to the community, so the sponsor wants to be known as a good corporate citizen. By aligning their brand with the life-changing work that you do, Sponsors can bask in the "halo effect."

5. Create a Compelling Sponsor Proposal - The sponsor proposal is the most important, but least understood document in the sponsor industry. If you want top-tier sponsors, you need a compelling sponsor proposal. It's also called the sponsorship deck or prospectus. This is basically a business plan and snapshot of the benefits of your property. The sponsor proposal contains the story of your property, mission statement, sponsor benefits, demographics, marketing plan, goals, media opportunities, advisory board and the sponsor fees.

If you want a bank loan, you need to fill out an application. If you want corporate sponsors, you need to submit a sponsor proposal. But you have to pay back bank loan. Sponsor money does not need to be paid back, however you need to provide quality and value to your sponsors.

6. Concentrate on Value, Not Expenses - The mistake that many people make is to calculate their expenses, then ask for that amount of money from a sponsor. Sponsorship is a value-based proposition. It's not based on expenses. What you provide has its own intrinsic value.

7. Have Experience (But Not Always Necessary!) - Sponsors want experience, but don't worry. If you don't have it, someone else does. Tell the sponsor about your previous experience in a related business. Surround yourself with key influencers on your advisory board. Tell the sponsor about leading-edge companies that you know or have worked with. If you have a new property (aka: business/brand), have a long-term marketing plan. You can sell the sponsors on your concept. I had never produced a live speaking event in my life, but I got Bank of America, Wal-Mart and IBM as my first sponsors. I had no track-record, but plenty of passion!

8. Make Integrity Part of Your Brand - Sponsors want to see that you have integrity and credibility. They will test you to see if you do what you say. Get them their information on time and arrive early to appointments. Keep in mind that you need to pass their unspoken tests to see if you can handle their brand image.

3 Benefits That You Can Offer Sponsors

Here are 3 different benefits you can offer corporate sponsors:

1. Web Site & Emails: You can put the sponsor logo on your web site, hyperlinks, and descriptions about your sponsor's company and how they help people. You can also include the sponsor in your email marketing and all marketing materials (i.e., brochure and other collateral).

2. Social Media: You can include sponsors in your Social Media profiles and incorporate their graphics in your company's description, fan pages, news feed, videos, photo galleries, etc.

3. Live Connections: Every time you speak, it's considered a live event in the sponsor world. Don't call what you do a speaking presentation. Call it a speaking and media tour. At your live events, you can give the sponsor 5 minutes of your talk, let them introduce you, include them in your signage and hand out their marketing information. When you do media, you can also mention the sponsor company. If you sell books and programs, you can include coupons and/or samples of the sponsor's products.

Follow Up With Sponsors:

Follow up can make or break you in the sponsor game. Make a follow up plan. I've seen many people *lose great sponsor deals because they lacked follow up skills.* When talking with a prospective sponsor, always make a follow up appointment. Confirm that appointment by email. If you're not strong in follow up, find someone who is.

Corporate sponsorship can give you the resources to skyrocket your speaking career. Sponsors have given me opportunities to do more speaking, travel the world, create my own events, do lots of media, and empower more people with my message. If I can do it, so can you. You have quality and value to offer sponsors. Dream big…and go out and get them!

About the Author: Linda Hollander is known as the *Wealthy Bag Lady.* She is the author of *Bags to Riches,* the founder of the Women's Small Business Expo and the President of Sponsor Concierge. Her corporate sponsors have included: Citibank, Fed Ex, Health Net, American Airlines, Bank of America, Staples, Marriott Vacation Club, Wal-Mart and IBM. Linda is also a sponsorship consultant, speaker and President of the International Sponsorship Association.

Contact Info:
Linda Hollander
www.WealthyBagLady.com
866-Women-Biz

CHAPTER TWENTY-THREE

10 Tips for Networking Your Way to On-going Revenue

By Lisa Orrell

Nowadays, most people seem to be solely focused on social networking *online*. And, yes, I know that we have covered a lot of social media networking and online marketing strategies in this book. However, while all of those are extremely powerful and worthwhile tools to use in this new era of business and technology, I find that many clients I work with tend to forget about *the other* type of networking; good old fashioned "live and in-person" networking by attending industry events and professional association mixers!

Quite honestly, I find that attending in-person networking events can typically yield me positive business results faster than online networking. Therefore, I make an effort to include in-person networking strategies in my business-building mix.

But, I also find that people are not that great at using their valuable in-person networking time wisely. So I often spend time giving my clients tips on networking at events so that they are comfortable attending them and can get the most out of their time doing so.

That said, here are 10 tips I recommend to make your in-person networking efforts a success:

1. Show-up with your business cards! People often forget their cards, or only bring a few, and that's embarrassing. Bring a good-sized stack with you so you don't run out. Some people you meet will ask for several because they may know other people who need your services.

2. Don't be shy. Remember, everyone is there to meet new people, so you are all in the same boat. Find someone standing alone or a small group of people, walk up, extend your hand (for a FIRM shake), smile and introduce yourself. It'll feel weird the first couple of times but people who network a lot are used to strangers approaching them. And if you say it's your first time attending the mixer, they'll normally want to help you meet other people.

3. Practice your 15-second "personal infomercial" before you arrive. When someone asks what you do, be able to explain your business in 15-seconds *or less.* DO NOT bore people with a long sales pitch or a bumbling explanation about your business.

4. You should take an interest in the people you meet first. It's common to blab on about yourself when you're nervous or trying to land business, so make a conscious effort to ask people questions *about them* and LISTEN to what they share closely.

5. Depending on the length of the mixer, try not to spend more than 5-10 minutes with each person. You're there to meet people! Now if you're really enjoying yourself with someone, and/or you're talking to what may be a potential client, maybe spend a bit more time. BUT, KEEP IN MIND, they may want to be moving on to meet more people, too, so don't monopolize their time. They might be too shy to excuse themselves, so be mindful of time, and watch their eyes and body language!

6. If alcohol is being served, don't overdo it. I've seen quite a few people start the event making a great impression and then, after a few drinks, they spiral downhill.

7. Make a lot of eye contact with people and smile! It's all about human contact, and smiling will draw people to you. Yet when most people get nervous they sit on the sidelines and hope people will come to them. A genuine, warm smile will relax people you meet and will make connecting with you more inviting.

8. Practice being a good conversationalist. Rather than just talk about you and your business (or theirs), have a few interesting questions memorized, and ask about kids, travel, previous jobs, pets, sports, current events, etc. Also, by *really listening to people* (which many people aren't great at!) questions will come up naturally that you can ask to keep the conversation going. And, personally, I avoid topics around religion and politics.

9. If someone approaches a group you're talking to, immediately extend your hand, smile, and make them feel welcome.

10. Send a hand written follow-up note to all the people you meet (mail them within 1-2 days after the event). The immediate thought is to send e-mail, but a card with a "Nice meeting you" note, sent via snail mail, makes a BIG impression on people... because people rarely send them nowadays!

Before I end this chapter, I'd also like to give you four suggestions on the *types* of networking groups and events you should consider looking into. Each of them serves a different purpose for building your business:

• I recommend joining one local group that has a variety of small business owner members from different industries. A good example of an organization like that is a Chamber of Commerce. I look at a Chamber as a place where some members can become clients and other members can become colleagues and support professionals that I recommend to people (i.e. lawyer, bookkeeper, hair salon owner, dentist, therapist, etc.). This type of "general" business association with a wide variety of small business owners is great for building your professional support database and getting referrals.

• The other type of group that I recommend joining is one that is made-up of other people *in your industry*. If you're a CPA, join a local professional association for Accountants. If you're a Life Coach, join a networking group for Coaches. There is a professional networking group and/or association for ANY industry and occupation you can think of. And if there isn't one in your area, start a Meet-Up Group of your own! I like networking with peers because we "speak the same language," share information to help each other, create products and events with each other, discuss new trends in our industry, and much more.

• Another networking group you should consider is one primarily made-up of *your target audience.* Obviously the purpose of networking with a group like this is to land clients. I have a client who is a Professional Baby Planner and her main target audience is first-time expecting Moms. So I advised her to attend local networking events for pregnant women. And, yes, there are many support and networking groups for expecting Moms! I also suggested that she offer to conduct free 30-minute seminars at the monthly mixers, and that strategy worked great for attracting new clients to her.

• The fourth place I suggest for in-person networking is to attend, or exhibit at, tradeshows that cater to your target audience. Booth rental space ranges from free to thousands of dollars, and that depends on the show. But I have exhibited at great smaller tradeshows where my booth rental was only $150 and I walked away with a significant amount of qualified leads. However, you don't have to be an exhibitor to make a tradeshow work for you. If the event is having speakers, submit a Speaker Proposal way ahead of time with a topic you can speak on. Or, you can simply attend the tradeshow and network with exhibitors and other attendees. Regardless, make sure you bring plenty of flyers or brochures about your business and tons of business cards with you!

Okay, now find some good association mixers and industry

events in your area (or even nationally), and try to attend at least 1-3 per month. There is a very good chance you'll reap the benefits of your networking efforts quickly, such as: see your connection database grow quickly; find new opportunities otherwise missed; meet new colleagues who can support you; and attracting new clients for on-going revenue!

LISA ORRELL

CHAPTER TWENTY-FOUR

Final Closing Comments from Lisa

If you're still not sure if creating a topic expert platform, or starting any other type of small business, is for you (because being self-employed on a full-time or part-time basis freaks you out), I suggest picking up a copy of an older, yet impactful, book: *Feel the Fear and Do It Anyway.*

We can't rely on the government to have the money and programs to support us into our golden years. So, unless you have a substantial retirement account and solid investments in-place, a major inheritance coming your way, adult children who can support you, or know without a doubt you'll win the lottery, your financial security is *in your hands.*

So the main goal of this book was to explain some ways *you can create more security for yourself by monetizing what you know.* I know it's packed with tons of info that may have your head spinning, but don't be overwhelmed! Just start by focusing on the info in Part One to begin developing *what* you could be a topic expert on. And once you are clear on that, go back to the other chapters and start planning your Business Model, and your Marketing, PR, Social Media and Sales efforts.

The key here, as with anything new, is just take the first step! And, in closing, I simply want to say best wishes for your success… and have fun!

All about Lisa Orrell, The Promote U Guru

"I love helping people accomplish their goals, especially if fear has been their biggest obstacle. 'Teaching' my clients effective marketing strategies is just one piece of the puzzle for making their business's successful...getting them to believe in themselves, push outside their comfort zones, think outside the box, and be consistent in their efforts, are also key components that I help clients achieve on a daily basis. And, to me, that is what makes my career as The Promote U Guru so rewarding."

~ Lisa Orrell,
The Promote U Guru, Author of this Book ...*and just an all-around lovable gal!*

CHAPTER TWENTY-FIVE

How Can Lisa Help Promote U?

As a Branding Expert, Marketing Consultant and Certified Success Coach with over 20-years of experience, here's an overview of what I can help you with. Some of my clients just need help with *a few things*, but many of them seek my help with MOST OF IT! And I offer a variety of Consulting Packages, with a wide range of pricing options to fit most budgets, so don't hesitate to contact me for more info.

BRANDING:

- Develop your unique Branding Platform, Positioning & Messaging

- Assess your current Branding Platform and improve it

- Assure your Branding (visual and written) is consistent across all of your marketing materials and outbound communications

- Position you as an Industry Thought Leader and/or Topic Expert to land media interviews; generate more clients; attract paid speaking opportunities; and (for Authors) increase book sales.

MARKETING/PR/SOCIAL MEDIA:

- Review your current marketing materials & provide feedback

- Identify marketing materials you need

- Create effective Sales & Marketing strategies (and assess any current efforts you may be implementing)

- Assess your current website and provide feedback (If you need a new website, I can help you determine the navigation, features & content. Plus, I'll provide feedback on the initial design concepts.)

- Write or edit copy for your website and marketing materials

- Create Virtual Book Tour strategies (for Authors)

- Determine (or improve) your Social Media strategy

- Develop your Social Media Marketing strategy (outside of your standard business use of: Twitter, Facebook, LinkedIn, YouTube, etc.)

- Develop strategies to attract and secure speaking engagements

- Create ideas for seminars, workshops, webinars & teleseminars

- Advise on your presentation pricing and policies/procedures for your speaking engagement contracts and proposals

- Strategize your product development (e-books, Special Reports, videos, etc.) to generate passive income

- Create a PR strategy, which includes: Creating Press Release topics; writing or editing your Press Release(s); how/where to deploy them; developing "topic" ideas to pitch the media; media outreach training; media interview tips; and much more!

SPEAKER & PRESENTATION CONSULTING:

Some of my clients already conduct seminars and workshops to attract customers, generate additional income from <u>paid</u> speaking engagements, and/or to sell their books or other products, but want to benefit more from what they do. And a lot of them *want to start speaking* for those same reasons. However, I have found that a majority of clients are NOT good at it…they need *speaker training and presentation advice!*

Here are the issues I see A LOT: Their PowerPoint presentations are a mess (visually, content and flow); or the presentation is "disorganized"; or their topics and titles lack appeal; or their "delivery/speaking" technique and style are boring; or they are clueless about up-selling the audience by providing special offers; *or all of the above.* Any ONE of those issues can cause your presentation to bomb and be ineffective.

Therefore, as a professional speaker myself, I offer special consulting packages *to assess and address* these common issues to help my clients **get the results they desire** from speaking! So, whether you have existing presentations, or <u>want to start speaking</u> to generate more revenue, I can help you on MANY levels.

PROFESSIONAL SUCCESS COACHING:

There are many times outside of my "branding and marketing consultation" where my clients face personal obstacles (confidence, time management, etc.), and require assistance with breaking through those barriers. And many of these *non-marketing* obstacles can prove to be more detrimental to building and growing a business, or career, than just about anything else. If you work with me, I will encourage you to share (honestly) any personal and professional issues you're facing so that we can work together in getting you through them. *We always want you moving forward; not stuck in one place!*

Lisa Orrell, CPC
The Promote U Guru
Branding Expert • Marketing Maven • Success Coach

Lisa holds a B.S. Degree in Advertising with a Minor in Marketing from San Jose State University. She started her first advertising agency when she was just 25-years-old, and continued to run her award-winning company for 20-years in Silicon Valley. During that time, her clients ranged from technology start-ups to Fortune 500 corporations, and she received 75+ prestigious national and international awards for Branding, Marketing and Strategic excellence.

But, after two decades of running her ad agency, Lisa decided to make a career shift. Today, in the next phase of her professional life, Lisa is highly respected as *The Promote U Guru*. She is an in-demand Branding Expert, Marketing Consultant and Certified Success Coach who works with: Entrepreneurs, small business owners, coaches, consultants, entertainers, academics, business executives, speakers and authors.

Lisa's clients and audiences benefit from her unique blend of being a 20-year veteran business owner, Marketing & Branding Expert, Certified Success Coach, Professional Speaker and Author. She personally understands what it takes to: create a unique Personal or Business Brand Platform; market and build a small business effectively; launch a speaker platform for additional income; develop products for revenue generation; and (for authors) promote and market a book effectively.

And, recently, Lisa was named *The Top 30 Most Influential Brand Gurus in the World* by BrandGurus.net. This professional organization selected top branding experts around the globe (who fit specific criteria) and then asked over 22,000 industry professionals to vote on the candidates they believed should make the final Top 30 List. Also, because of her extensive brand notoriety and experience, in 2011 Lisa was asked by the International Coach Academy (ICA) to be a lead Instructor for a variety of Branding & Marketing courses in their *Business Base Camp Program.* ICA is a world-renowned ICF-accredited coach training certification academy, and their *Business Base Camp Program* was developed to help new and seasoned Coaches build a thriving coaching practice.

As a professional speaker, Lisa's popular in-person and on-line presentations consistently sell out on topics such as: Branding, Marketing, PR, Publicity, Book Marketing & Publishing, and Social Media. Plus, Lisa offers Speaker & Presentation assessment and consultation services for individuals who are currently speaking, *or* aspire to, for revenue generation.

In addition to her speaking, consulting, and teaching, Lisa is also the author of two top-selling business books on Amazon, *Millennials into Leadership* (written for Gen Y about how to be young, effective leaders at work) and *Millennials Incorporated* (how to recruit, manage and retain Gen Y). Her expertise on these topics attracts well-known corporations and colleges to also hire Lisa for seminars and workshops. You can learn more about this aspect of her professional life by visiting her "other" business website at: TheOrrellGroup.com.

Based on her business expertise, Lisa has been interviewed by, or written articles for, countless media, including: ABC, MSNBC, NPR, *The Wall Street Journal, The New York Times, TIME, U.S. News & World Report, Cosmo,* China's *HerWorld Magazine,* WomenEntrepreneur.com, CareerBuilder.com, Monster.com and BNET.com.

Visit Lisa's Website for Information about Her Promote U Business Building Boot Camp Tele-Course and Her Exclusive Promote U Mastermind Club!

www.PromoteUGuru.com

Lisa provides tons of FREE Marketing & Business advice and information through her Social Media Networks, so be sure to join her online at:

Twitter: @PromoteUGuru
Fan Page: Facebook.com/PromoteUGuru
Blog: PromoteUGuru.com/Blog
YouTube Channel: YouTube.com/ThePromoteUGuru

Contact Lisa Today to Promote U or to Speak at Your Next Event!

Lisa Orrell, CPC
The Promote U Guru
Branding Expert • Marketing Maven • Success Coach
Professional Speaker & Author
Lisa@PromoteUGuru.com
www.PromoteUGuru.com
1-888-254-LISA

LISA ORRELL

CPSIA information can be obtained at www.ICGtesting.com
Printed in the USA
LVOW121219011212

309630LV00003B/227/P